A Covert from the Storm

or, the Fearful Encouraged in Times of Suffering

By Nathaniel Vincent

A Covert from the Storm or, the Fearful Encouraged in Times of Suffering
By Nathaniel Vincent

Edited and updated by C. Matthew McMahon and Therese B. McMahon
Transcribed by Blake Gentry

Published by Puritan Publications
A Ministry of A Puritan's Mind
4101 Coral Tree Circle #214
Coconut Creek, FL 33073
www.puritanshop.com
www.apuritansmind.com
www.puritanpublications.com

This Print Edition, 2012
Electronic Edition, 2012
Manufactured in the United States of America

ISBN: 978-1-938721-69-4
eISBN: 978-1-938721-68-7

TABLE OF CONTENTS

MEET NATHANIEL VINCENT

[Vincent's Portrait by John White (1681) from the National Portrait Gallery]

Nathaniel Vincent (1639?-1697), nonconformist puritan divine, was probably born in Cornwall about 1639 (*cf. epist. Dedication* to *A Present for such as have been Sick*).

His father, John Vincent (1591-1646), son and heir of Thomas Vincent of Northill, Cornwall, born in 1591, matriculated from New College, Oxford, on Dec. 15, 1609, became a student at Lincoln's Inn in 1612, and, afterwards taking orders, was beneficed in Cornwall. Of nonconformist leanings, he was driven there by his bishop, as well as from so many other livings that it was said no two of his seven children were born in the same county. Coming to London in 1642, he was nominated by the committee of the Westminster assembly to the rich rectory of Sedgefield, Durham, but died after holding it but two years, in 1646. His widow, Sarah Vincent, petitioned on Nov. 1, 1656 and in April 1657 for 60£ which her husband had lent to the parliament (Cal. *State Papers*, Dom. 1656, pp. 146, 147, 185, 191, 329; Addit. MS. 15671, cf. ff. 38, 42, 55, 69, 114, 124, 140, 148, 150, 219, 227, 238, 251). Their eldest son, John, who inherited his grandfather's estate of Northill, is confused by Mr. Wood with a son of Augustine Vincent (*Athenæ Oxon.* vol. i. p. xxxv). The second son, Thomas, is separately noticed.

Nathaniel, the third son, entered Oxford University as a chorister on Oct. 18, 1648, at age 10. He matriculated from Corpus Christi College on March 28, 1655, graduated with a B.A. from Christ Church on March 13, 1655-6, M. A.

on June 11, 1657, and was chosen chaplain of Corpus Christi College. He was appointed by Cromwell as one of the first fellows of Durham University, but never lived there. At twenty he was preaching at Pulborough, Sussex, and at twenty-one he was ordained and presented to the rectory of Langley Marish, Buckinghamshire. There he was ejected on St. Bartholomew's day, 1662, after which he lived three years as chaplain to Sir Henry and Lady Blount at Tittenhanger, Hertfordshire. About 1666 Vincent went to London. There his preaching at once attracted attention, and a meeting-house was shortly built for him in Farthing Alley, Southwark, where he gathered a large congregation. In spite of fines and rough handling by soldiers sent to drag him from his pulpit, he continued boldly preaching during the stormy times. In July 1670, soon after his marriage, he was confined in the Marshalsea prison. He was removed to the Gatehouse, Westminster, on Aug. 22 (*cf.* Cal. State Papers, Dom., Addenda, 1660-70, p. 546). He remained six months in prison. In 1682 he was again arrested, brought before magistrates at Dorking, and sentenced to three years' imprisonment, after which he was to be banished from the country. A flaw, however, was perceived in the indictment, and, after the section expenditure of 200£, Vincent was released, but so weakened from illness that he was long unable to preach (Letter to his Congregation, 24

June 1683). He was again arrested in February 1686, this time on an improbable charge of being concerned in Monmouth's rebellion (Wood, Life and Times, ed. Clark, iii. 179). Some of his books were written in prison; thus "his pen was going when his tongue could not."

Vincent died suddenly on June 22, 1697, in the fifty-ninth year of his age. He was buried at Bunhill Fields; (see *Inscriptions on Tombs in Bunhill* Fields, 1717, p. 34). His funeral sermon was preached by Nathaniel Taylor.

Wood's *encomium* on Vincent is unusually high, "He was of smarter, more brisk, and florid parts than most of his dull and sluggish fraternity can reasonably pretend to; of a facetious and jolly humour, and a considerable scholar."

The *works* of Nathaniel Vincent are as follows:

1. *The Doctrine of Conversion*, or, *The Conversion of a Sinner Explained and Applied*, London, 1669, 8vo; with which is published 2. *The Day of Grace* (same date). 3. *A Covert from the Storm*, London, 1671, 8vo (written in prison). 4. *The Spirit of Prayer*, London, 1674, 8vo; republished, 1677, 8vo; 5th edit. 1699; other edits. Saffron Walden, ed. J. H. Hopkins, 1815, London, 1825. 5. *A Heaven or Hell upon Earth*, London, 1676,

8vo. 6. *The Little Child's Catechism*, whereunto is added several Short Histories, 1681, 12mo. 7. *The True Touchstone*, London, 1681, 8vo. 8. *The More Excellent Way*, London, 1684. 9. *A Warning given to secure Sinners*, London, 1688, 8vo. 10. *The Principles of the Doctrine of Christ: a Catechism*, London, 1691, 8vo. 11. *A Present for such as have been Sick* (sermons preached after his recovery from sickness), London, 1693. 12. *The Cure of Distractions in attending upon God*. 13. *The Love of the World cured*. 14. *Worthy Walking*. The dates of the last three do not appear. Sermons by Vincent are in Annesley's *Continuation of Morning Exercises*, London, 1683, and in his *Casuistical Morning Exercises*, London, 1690; reprinted in vols. iv., v., and vi. of Nichols's edition, London, 1814-5, 8vo. Vincent was much in request for preaching funeral sermons; five or six were printed in quarto. He edited the *Morning Exercise against Popery* (London, 1675, 4to), twenty- five sermons preached in his pulpit at Southwark by eminent divines.

For further study:

Clark's *Indexes*, vol. ii. pt. i. p. 280, pt. ii. p. 308; Foster's *Alumni* (1500-1714); Neal's Puritans, iii. 521; Calamy's *Continuation*, i. 30; *Alumni Westmon.* p. 129; Burrows's *Visitation*, pp. 171, 173, 369, 477; Bloxam's *Reg. of Magd. Coll.* v. 208; Palmer's *Nonconf. Mem.* i. 304; Wood's *Athenae Oxon.* iv. 617; Wilson's *Hist. of Diss. Churches*, iv. 304 (this is the most accurate account); Cal. *State Papers*, Dom. Add. 1660-70 pp. 273, 388, 464, 1671 p. 556; Taylor's Funeral Sermon, 1697, 4to; Wood's *Life and Times* (Oxford Hist. Soc.), ii. 561; *Hist. MSS. Comm.* 11th *Rep. App.* p. 46; *Notes and Queries*, 2nd ser. ix. 267.

Taken in part from the National Dictionary of Biography, public domain.

[ORIGINAL TITLE PAGE]

A

COVERT

FROM THE

STORM

Or

The Fearful Encouraged
in Times of

SUFFERING;

FROM

Revelation 2:10, "Fear none of those things which thou shalt
suffer; behold the devil shall cast some of you into prison, that
ye may be tried, and ye shall have tribulation ten days; be thou
faithful unto death, and I will give thee a crown of life."

By NATHANIEL VINCENT,
a preacher and prisoner of Jesus Christ, and written during his
close confinement, when few could come to him but his God,
who yet abundantly made up the lack of other company.

LONDON,
Printed in the year 1671.

DEDICATION

To him that is higher than the highest, and will shortly come to judge the world in righteousness. Most mighty Lord! A prisoner approaches to your footstool, and not without some confidence, because he is confined not for evil doing, but for well doing. That which men account his crime, you have made his duty, and by doing this he has incurred their displeasure; but he hopes he has avoided your displeasure. He was willing to cast the new over a great many, that the more might be taken, and by being taken, set indeed at liberty. He was desirous that the subjects of your kingdom might be multiplied, therefore he truly thinks however men may censure it, you do not call it rashness or zeal not according to knowledge.

Since you have commanded your messengers to go into the highways, and as many as they find to bid to the marriage, since you lay an injunction on them, to preach the Gospel to every creature, surely you never did intend that their compassion and care should be confined to a very few. O therefore that every five of them that hear your voice and follow you might be increased into many thousands! Thin congregations are a lamentable sight. Let them therefore fly as a cloud, and as doves to their windows.

Incline the hearts of magistrates to pity and moderation; let their sword be drawn only against those that are malefactors truly so called, not against such as would gladly be at work for you, and turning many to righteousness. Convince them that it will be the design and desire of a godly ministry to make their hearers better subjects to their earthly rulers, as well as to the King of saints.

Your prisoner, who is in this gate-house doing your will and pleasure, earnestly petitions for his liberty. He deserves to be laid aside, but desires to be used. He would gladly have the prison door open to let him out, but is a great deal more earnest to have the pulpit door open to let him in, that he might again be preaching your Gospel. He longs to be warning the secure, who do not see the sword drawn out against them; to be stopping the madmen who are making such hast to eternal destruction; to be inviting the miserable to mercy, and the lost to a Savior. Where is your zeal and your strength, O Lord, and the founding of your bowels, and your mercies! Are they restrained? O pity immortal souls that are going to hell by droves; and in some places, the pastors are so far from hindering, that being exemplary for looseness and impiety, they go before them to perdition.

Your prisoner blesses you that he ever had the honor to be in bonds for you. The worst of you, even your cross, is not at all to be disliked. The enlargements of his heart have been greater, than when he was at liberty; his peace has been more perfect. Your presences is so sweet, that he would go to any place to have more of it. You have given in that grace which is glory begun. He confidently believes this jail will make him more fit for the glorious liberty of your children; and that he shall praise you forever for what he has endured.

Your servant can say it with boldness before you, that he honors the authority you have set over him; he has put others in mind to be subject to principalities and powers; to be ready for every good work; and remembers it is his own duty to be thus subject. Only he has preached contrarily to the magistrate's command, because your command is so express for preaching; and you press it on pastors, as they love you to feed your lambs, to feed your sheep.

O you dreadful and heart-searching Judge! Cause the integrity of your nonconforming servants to shine so brightly as to break through all unreasonable prejudices! Let their righteousness be brought forth as the light, and their judgment as the noon day, that that severity may be at length ashamed of itself that is used towards them. O hasten your second appearing, that the secrets of hearts may be discovered, and that it may be made manifest before men and angels, who have worshipped you the rightest way; who mostly have sought you, and least themselves.

Your servant being taken off from preaching, was

14

willing to be some way beneficial to your Church; therefore his pen has been going when his tongue could not. And if souls are edified and encouraged, if your kingdom and Name and glory are in any way advanced by this writing, then the highest end will be attained, which is aimed at by him, who is not, who would not be his own, but by millions of obligations is engaged to be

Yours eternally,

NATHANIEL VINCENT

EPISTLE TO THE READER

To the readers, especially those that were not my hearers.

Readers.

Should arguments be used with the tossed in a tempest to put into a haven, or with the pursued by the avenger to fly to a sanctuary? Their danger is the best rhetoric to persuade them to that which is for their own security (*self-love*). And if your danger was more deeply and rightly apprehended, you would hasten to the Lord, whose Name is a strong tower, and who has promised to be a hiding from the wind, a covert from the tempest, as rivers of water in a dry place, and as the shadow of a great rock in a weary land, (Isaiah 32:2).

The devil has great wrath because he knows that he has only a short time. We in this latter age of the world must expect more furious assaults from him, because the Day of Judgment, to which he is reserved, is coming quickly. His instruments are enraged, and drive on furiously. But what is all their force and power, to the strength of that Almighty Lord, who if you leave to him, and trust in him, has covenanted to uphold you? How inconsiderable is their anger, when your believing thoughts have dwelt a little on his kindness and compassion!

Do not be frightened at the cross of Christ, it will, when felt and sweetened, be found to be no more of a burden to you, than wings are to the bird flying in the air, or sails to the ship cutting through the sea; it will be a means to mend your pace, and make you run swifter in your race, towards the prize of the high calling of God. If your Lord has not known the easiness and usefulness of his yoke, he would never have required you to have taken it on yourself.

I have preached much to your encouragement. Now I am taken off, a sad silence is imposed on me. Only my mouth is still open to the Lord for you, that you may stand perfect and complete in all the will of God. I could not have satisfied either you or myself, unless in this my restraint and retirement, I had written something that might be a furtherance to your faith and joy in this hour of temptation. The blessing of the Father of spirits go along with this book! O that believers may be strengthened and refreshed by it! And if enemies read it with an ill mind, the author wishes that by reading it, their minds may be changed, and for their own sakes as well as his made better.

Nathaniel Vincent

A COVERT FROM THE STORM

"Fear none of those things which thou shalt suffer; behold the devil shall cast some of you into prison, that ye may be tried, and ye shall have tribulation ten days; be thou faithful unto death, and I will give thee a crown of life," (Revelation 2:10).

A light is hung up at the porch of this book, which is so very serious. The first three chapters are easier to be understood than those that follow. Here the waters of the sanctuary are only up to the head, but presently they grow so deep that the tallest must be gladly to swim. I am persuaded that one reason why the Holy Spirit speaks so sublimely, is that man, when he reads, may sometimes lay aside the book, and cry, Ὦ βάθος O the depth! And being more humbly sensible of his own ignorance and weaknesses, may pray with greater earnestness, that the Spirit who was the Inspirer would also be the Interpreter of the revelation.

Seven epistles, or letters, dated from heaven, indicted by the Son of God, are sent to the seven Churches of Asia. He who knew their works, owns what is right, taxes what was amiss, and calls to repentance and amendment, and charges them to hold fast to those good things which they had received, as being a treasure highly worth keeping. The

Captain of their salvation encourages them to act like men, that overcoming they might be crowned in the end.

The text I have chosen lies in the epistle sent to the Church in *Smyrna*. They were poor in the world, and yet rich towards God; and it is not unlikely that for the securing of their spiritual riches, as to worldly things they had been impoverished. Christ knew their works, and as their works, so likewise their tribulation; he also knew how to support them under the heaviest and most pressing burdens, no, to render all their troubles as advantageous, by conducing to their more perfect purity and peace; and therefore bids them in no wise to be afraid, "Fear none of those things which thou shalt suffer." Our Lord came to deliver, not only from the sting of death, and from the curse of the cross and affliction, but from the fear of both.

THREE PARTS TO THE TEXT

The words may be analyzed or resolved into three *parts*:

First, here is a general encouragement against all kinds of suffering. "Fear none of those things which thou shalt suffer."

Secondly, among other sufferings, imprisonment is specified and foretold, where we take notice of the following.

1. Who is the procuring cause of imprisonment, and he is the devil. 2. The persons imprisoned, "Some of you." All the saints shall not be in bonds together. 3. The end of their imprisonment, which their God aims at in permitting it; it is "that they may be tried." 4. Although they have tribulation, it shall not be long-lived, for "it shall last but ten days," that is a very short season.

Thirdly, we have a strict charge given, "Be thou faithful," and that even to "the death:" Perseverance must run parallel with our lives.

Fourthly, a sure and glorious promise, persuading to this faithfulness and enduring to the end, "I will give thee a crown of life." Here is a crown, a word that carries great dignity and advancement. This crown is a *crown of life*, or a living crown. The garland that is put on the heads of triumphant saints will never wither, their crown will never fade, there will be no death to throw it off again once they have received it. This crown shall be given to show that what they do, or can do, bears no proportion to such a reward. Neither their active nor passive obedience is meritorious. Grace, *grace*, must be written around the crown of glory, because it is freely bestowed. "I will give this crown," says Christ. "I who have purchased it by my death, who have it in my keeping, who am the Lord of glory, and alive forevermore."

NINE POINTS OF DOCTRINE

The text is very fruitful, and affords several very excellent and useful points of doctrine. I shall raise these nine, which flow naturally from the words, and insist on them all.

1. He that will be a saint will be a sufferer.

2. No sufferings should cause the saints to be afraid.

3. Among other troubles, some believers endure bonds and imprisonment.

4. The devil is the imprisoner of believers.

5. That saints are imprisoned, that they may be tried.

6. The tribulation of believers will not last always, after ten days, that is a short time, a period will be put to it.

7. Whatever sufferings a Christian is exposed to, he must be faithful.

8. A Christian's faithfulness must run parallel with his life, he must be steadfast to the very death.

9. On those who continue faithful to the death, Christ will certainly bestow a crown of life and immortality.

THE FIRST DOCTRINE

The first doctrine. *He that will be a saint, will be a sufferer.* The Spirit speaks hardly anything more expressly than he does this truth. The apostle tells what afflictions and persecutions he met with, and peremptorily affirms that none shall escape. Persecution shall be met with, if not one kind, in another. Drops shall fall on every saint, though some may be wet with greater showers. "But thou hast fully known my doctrine, manner of life, purpose, faith, longsuffering, charity, patience, persecutions, afflictions, which came unto me at Antioch, at Janium, and Lystra, what persecutions I endured there. But out of them all the Lord delivered me. yea and all that will live godly in Christ Jesus shall suffer persecution," (2 Timothy 3:10-12). Also consult, "Confirming the souls of the disciples, and exhorting them to continue in the faith, and we must through many tribulations enter into the kingdom of God," (Acts 14:22). The journey's end is glorious, but the way that leads to it is tough, for it lies through many tribulations. Self-denial and the cross are doctrines which Christ preached to all his followers. "And he said unto them all, if any man will come after me, let him deny himself, and take up his cross and follow me," (Luke 9:23).

WHY DOES THE LORD CAUSE SAINTS TO SUFFER?

Two things are to be inquired of here. One is, what is the reason of these dispensations? Or, why the Lord suffers those he loves, to be so exercised?

First, from where do the sufferings of saints arise? They are both from the god of this world, and from the world itself. Earth and hell both combine to trouble the heirs of heaven, as they are going to their inheritance.

1. The saint's sufferings arise from the god of this world. So Satan in Scripture is called. He commands the generality of the world, who are at his service, and are led by him at his pleasure, and those whom he cannot rule, he is resolved, when he can, to molest and disquiet. The devil began in times of old; righteous Abel felt the effects of his enmity and hatred; and he continues this persecuting trade to this very hour. And until the whole body of Christ is taken up where the Head is, Satan will be as a thorn, to pierce and trouble them.

SATAN PERSECUTING THE SAINTS

It will not be amiss to examine the matter further; and to search into the cause, why Satan so endeavors to load the saints with sufferings.

1. The devil bears an implacable hatred to the saints of the Lord Jesus. He would gladly have killed Christ from the birth; and incited Herod to make such weeping and lamentation in Rome, because of the children that were so inhumanely butchered, (Matthew 2). Our Lord was tempted by the devil, (Matthew 4) who would have gladly soiled the

second, as he had done the first Adam; but he could not prevail. The devil is said to have put it into the heart of Judas to betray Christ. All which plainly shows his hatred of the Son of God. The works of Christ and of Satan are quite contrary. Satan's work is to murder and destroy; therefore he has his name, "Apollyon," (Revelation 9:11). But Christ's work is to save. The Son of God was manifested to this very end, that he might destroy the works of this Destroyer; and the Son of God has gotten the victory, "He hath spoiled principalities and powers, and made a show of them openly, triumphing over them in his cross," (Colossians 2:15). He is now ascended on high, and is at his Father's right hand. And the old Dragon, being full of wrath, to see him so exalted, spits his venom at the members, which are in his reach, for the Head's sake. And surely our Lord will look on himself as the more obliged to stand by his suffering servants, since it is for his sake partly, that this adversary is so liberal of his arrow, and shoots so many at them.

2. The devil is full of envy at believers themselves. As soon as he ever had sinned; presently the chains of darkness were clamped on him; he was immediately cast down to hell, with no patience being shown, no pity extended, no means of recovery offered. "God spared not the angels that sinned, but cast them down to hell, and delivered them into chains and darkness to be reserved unto judgment," (2 Peter 2). But

believers, though by nature are the children of wrath and disobedience, are pitied, pardoned, adopted, saved. A remedy is provided, and that remedy is made effectual through the application of it, to their recovery and the recovery of their lost blessedness. Now this fills Satan with envy, which is both his sin and torture, and envy stirs him up to do what mischief he is able to do.

3. The devil dislikes holiness wherever he finds it. He indeed hates all the children of men, but those that are sanctified and renewed, in a special manner. As he is utterly destitute of, so he utterly detests and abhors the image of God, which shows the fearful deprivation of his nature. It is no wonder he runs to the utmost length of his chain to harm the saints, "who have put off the old, and put on the new man, which after God is created in righteousness and true holiness," (Ephesians 4:24). Sin is arrived at its full growth. It has come to its perfection in the devil. Holiness is struck at by him, and he endeavors to discourage and hinder wherever he finds it. Those who resemble Satan in this, the measure of their iniquity is more full than they are aware of.

4. The devil designs by the persecuting of the saints, to promote his interest and kingdom. This prince of darkness is a very proud spirit. He would, by his good will, have the whole world to be his slaves and vessels. How he rages when any of whom he led captive are rescued from him! He is sedulous to

establish his throne and principality. O that saints were as zealous and diligent to advance the honor and interest of the King of saints! The devil hopes to promote his kingdom, not only by flattering sinners into his subjection, but also by affrighting them from the service of another lord.

FIVE WAYS SATAN GETS THE ADVANTAGE

There are five ways by which Satan is likely to be advantaged in times of *suffering:*

1. He is likely to take advantage by discouraging the weak in faith. He hopes that those who have weak hands and feeble knees will not easily get over those stumbling blocks, which are cast in their way in times of trouble. And if their hearts faint and fail, not only they themselves, but religion also loses its ground; and what ground is lost, the devil gains. He set on Peter when he was weak, and how far did he prevail? Peter falls most shamefully, and his fall cost him dearly; and how was the prejudice against Christ in the high priest's hall increased when one of his followers, thus with cursing and swearing, utterly denied him? Satan desires to have weak saints especially, that he may sift them as wheat. It is well that our Lord prays for them, that their faith may not fail in the hour of temptation.

2. Satan is likely to take advantage by making the temporaries fall away. He knows that the sun of persecution shining hot will scorch the seed that is sown and springs up on stony ground, (Matthew13:21). Temporary believers are quickly offended at Christ, and become unbelievers again. If a storm arises, they will leave the ship where Christ is, and loving carnal ease and a safe skin will put in to the next harbor. Let Christ be alone, if he will, in a tempest, and they will not then accompany him. And when many of these unfound disciples forsake the Lord, carnal hearts are more confirmed and hardened against him, as if it were unsafe and consequently a very unwise part to be of the number of his followers. The going away of temporary believers is very likely to hinder others from engaging to such a Master, who is so much deserted.

3. Satan is likely to take advantage in the times of suffering, by staving off those that are outside from coming in, and closing with Christ Jesus. When any begin to think of themselves, to consider their ways, and to mind salvation, the devil, especially in the day of calamity, fills their minds with such suggestions as these: that the cross of Christ is heavy; that it is dreadful to be hated of all men; that tribulation will pinch their flesh; that name, relations, credit, estate, and even perhaps life may be called for, as soon as Christ is closed with. And by this he strangely and strongly prevails on fearful and

corrupted nature. You had better, says Satan, understand when you are well and keep yourselves so; you had better live in peace and plenty, as the most of those about you do, than be singular in your way, and by that singularity make so many enemies, and pull down so many troubles on your heads. And truly the flesh has an open ear to such counsel, though it is very unreasonable and pernicious.

4. Satan is likely to take advantage in the time of suffering by lessening the saint's number. He does not care how many of these are cut off; he delights in the high and crying sin of those who are the saint's destroyers; and he knows that when believers are cut off, though he cannot trouble them, they cannot trouble him any longer by undermining his kingdom, as they did before. Saints, whose faith and love and hope set them above the fear of sufferings, are people whom the devil fears, as well as hates; therefore he wishes that he was rid of them. These will hearten and strengthen their brethren to stand fast in the Lord; these consequently are the marks at which he aims, and would gladly quite run them down to the very grave by tribulation.

5. Satan is likely to take advantage in the time of suffering by hindering the preaching and progress of the Gospel. Where persecution is vehement, vision grows rare; in those places where the joyful sound, the glad tidings of peace, used to be heard, there is a sad silence. The prophets are

driven into corners, and not suffered to cry aloud to sinners, to awaken them and turn them from darkness to light, and from the power of Satan to God. And when faithful laborers are thrown aside, Satan expects a plentiful harvest.

GOD USES EVIL FOR GOOD

Thus the devil aims at the promoting of his kingdom by striking at the saints. But the Lord commonly at last out-shoots him with his own bow, and makes these sufferings tend to the sufferer's good, and the Gospel's glory and increase. God can accomplish his ends by means that seem contrary; he can make Satan and persecutors serve his Son by enlarging his borders, which they thought and hoped to have narrowed. He can thrust forth (so the word in the original Greek, ἐκβάλῃ, signifies) laborers into his harvest again. And though men and devils stand to hinder their entrance and working, if the Lord thrusts them in, in they shall go, and work with more power and success than ever.

2. The saint's sufferings arise, as from the god of this world, so from the world itself. What Christ said concerning the Jews who went about to kill him, may be applied to those who are the troublers of his members, "They are of their father the devil, and the lusts of their father they will do," (John 8:44). He is a liar and a murderer, and so are they. They first

raise lies of believers, confidently affirming them to be rebellious. Seditious enemies to the kingdoms (though indeed the pillars of the nations where they live) having lied against them, they endeavor their ruin; having misrepresented them, they fall on them. They lie in saying, the saints are not fit to live, and then they strive to root them out of the land of the living. Thus they make nothing of transgressing at once both the sixth and the ninth commandment.

WHY MEN OF THE WORLD TROUBLE THE SAINTS

Now the reason which moves the men of this world to trouble the saints of God is *fourfold*:

1. The saints are not of the world. Our Lord speaks this way to his disciples, "If ye were of the world, the world would love his own, but because ye are not of the world, but I have chosen you out of the world, therefore the world hateth you," (John 15:19). Again, he speaks to the same purpose. "I have given them thy word, and the world hath hated them," the reason is, "because they are not of the world, even as I am not of the world," (John 17:14). Believers are unlike the men of the world, and this unlikeness is the ground of dislike. They do not dare to be careless of their souls, fearless of God, prodigal of the day of grace, as the world is. They are not conformed to this world, but transformed by the renewing of their minds,

and they prove what is good, the acceptable and the perfect will of God, (Romans 12:2). And truly the world is a great enemy to all of them that are non-conformists to its manners, although its manners are so exceedingly vain and sinful.

2. The saints are of God. And the men of the world, who are God haters, it is no wonder if they hate the saints likewise. *Visam for a savit in umbram.* Some beasts have such and antipathy to man, that they will run at his picture when they see it. In like manner, the world cannot endure those who have the image of God resplendent and shining in them. "Abel was hated because his works were righteous," (1 John 3:12). It is prodigiously strange that believers should be abhorred, because they are beautified with grace, and be hated because they are lovely.

3. The saints are a conviction to the consciences of the ungodly. It is said that Herod feared John the Baptist, because he was a just man and holy. Herod's conscience was struck with an awe by the majesty and beauty that appeared in the conversation of that burning and shining light. The holiness of John made Herod's wickedness the more apparent; and at last, he makes an end of him who so much disturbed him in his filthy and unlawful pleasures. Wicked men's consciences reproach them, because they are so unlike believers, though it is not unusual. Do you not see, says the conscience, how watchful the saints are, lest they enter into temptation? Do

you not see how they pray, how they strive, and how they live? Certainly you are in danger of the same hell, which they endeavor to avoid; and capable of the same kingdoms, which they use such violence to take. And by such language as this their false peace is entrenched on; they cannot sin with such freedom and delight, but the secret and condemning whispers of conscience, sour and lessen their pleasure. And this exceedingly raises their color; and like so many wolves, they fall on the harmless sheep of Christ, which live among them.

4. The saints act contrary to the perverse wills and inclinations of the wicked ones. They make conscience of obeying that injunction, "That he no longer lives the rest of his time in the flesh, to the lusts of men, but to the will of God." They are taught to not follow a multitude, and to judge that way to be unsafe and leading to ruin, which is the broadest and most crowded with passengers. They do not dare to run with others to all excess of riot, and on this score they are spoken evil of. Two things make the saints to be maligned by the men of the world; the saints hate what the men of the world love, and vilify what the men of the world adore.

1. They hate what the men of the world love. Believers' hatred of sin is universal, they strike at sin in themselves and others; they cannot patiently see such a cursed thing served by so many; they testify of its evil and destructive nature, and hereby though undeservedly, contract the ill will of those who

prefer their sins before their souls, and will by no means let their lusts go, though these lusts of theirs are such sure hindrances to their eternal happiness.

2. The saints vilify what the man of the world adores. As the Ephesians of old stood up for their goddess Diana, so the worldly-minded cry out, "Great is the mammon of unrighteousness." But believers trample on this idolized clay, they call it as it is, "Vanity and vexation of spirit," and are not afraid to let the earthly-minded know that it would have been better for them to have never come into the world at all, than to have nothing but the things of the world to be their portion.

You see now from where the sufferings of the saints arise, from the world, and from the god of the world.

GOD PERMITS THE EXERCISE OF HIS SAINTS TO SUFFER

In the second place we are to inquire, wherefore it is said that God permits the saints who are so dear to him, to be so exercised with sufferings.

1. Saints are exercised with suffering, that pride may be hidden from them. The sin of pride cleaves close, stands stiffly, and is not easily pulled down. A mighty hand is gladly to be laid on us, to keep our spirits low; and that mighty hand of God is a good hand, when, as the apostle speaks, we humble

ourselves under it. Sufferings make us often to reflect on sin, and to be the more affected by our guilt and vileness. Our weakness then likewise becomes more apparent; we see how assuredly we should sink, if an arm from heaven were not stretched forth to sustain us. And when we see our vileness and our weakness, we shall not think ourselves to be too good to suffer. We shall not through the haughtiness of our hearts, fret and be impatient under our loads; thus to do, is unreasonable, because infinitely more than we feel has been deserved; and the way to force the Lord to withdraw, whose presence is our staff and comfort. Sufferings being sanctified are hugely efficacious to our humiliation; bearing the yoke will tame our spirits, and "make us to put our mouths in the dust, if so be there may be hope," (Lamentations 3:29).

2. Saints are exercised with sufferings that they may be proved. Their faith and love and other graces, which are much more precious than gold, which perishes, are tried by the fire of afflictions, and abiding the fire will be found to praise and honor and glory, at the appearing of Jesus Christ, (1 Peter 1:7). It is a sign their grace is sincere indeed, if they follow the Lamb, though he leads them through the fire and water; their faith is strong, or else it would fail; their love is ardent, or else it would cool; they are the Lord Christ's, not only by profession, but by a read incorporation and spiritual union, or else tribulation would cause a separation. The accuser of the

brethren says perhaps to the Lord concerning believers, "Let man but touch what they have, let them be but exposed to suffering for thee, and they will presently deny thee." But when they prove steadfast as a rock in the midst of the most boisterous waves; when they will part with anything rather than their integrity, their sincerity is hereby tried and made manifest, and Satan's accusation is evidently proved to be a false one.

3. Saints are exercised with sufferings in order to their refining. Though they are not reprobate silver, yet much dross notwithstanding is mixed with the right metals; here it follows that the furnace of tribulation is needful. How do believers bestir themselves to keep in with God, when the world frowns and threatens and strikes at them? O then the folly of backsliding is very visible; how do they cry to have all those wide breaches that sin has made, closed and made up again! How do their spirits make a diligent search after everything that defiles, and which may prove to be a dark and uncomfortable cloud between the Lord and them. They are more than ordinarily earnest to have lust slain. And they profess that persecution will be esteemed a privilege, if it conduces to more perfect purity; and that they will kiss the rod that drives sin and folly far away from them. As the promises of support, so the promises of sanctification are often pleaded, in which God engages, "to cleanse them from

all their filthiness, to save them from all their uncleannesses, to give them his spirit, and to cause them to walk in his statutes, and to observe his judgments, and do them," (Ezekiel 36:25-26). The saints in distress hunger and thirst after righteousness, and the Lord satisfies that hunger by degrees. And the more they are freed from sin, their sufferings are the sweeter.

4. Saints are exercised with sufferings, that they may be weaned from things visible. Troubles are as much gall put on the world's breasts to wean us from it. In time of tribulation, the Lord, not only by his word, but by his providence, speaks to us after this manner, "Arise, this is not your rest, build not your rest here, the whole forest is sold to death, and every tree must shortly come down." It is in the time of peace usually that the world insinuates itself; in trouble its emptiness is more easily discerned. As believers are crucified to the world, so the world is *crucified to them*, (Galatians 6:14). They behold the world as that which sin has brought a curse on, and therefore to be watched against, lest it prove a snare; and then they look on the world with such a kind eye as the Jews did on Christ in his examination, "They see no form nor comeliness in it, that they should desire it," (Isaiah 53). Believers in the evil day, beside their hard usage from the world, which makes them less to like it, have more affecting thoughts of eternity and the world to come. And on these

things which are temporal grow contemptibleness, and are not counted worth a look. "Whilst we look not at the things which are see, but at the things that are not seen; and not without reason, for the things that are seen are temporal, but the things that are not seen are eternal," (2 Corinthians 4:18).

5. Saints are exercised with sufferings that they may be fitted for and long for the inheritance that is above. By sufferings they are made conformable to their Head, and are perfected and ripened more and more for glory. Therefore, afflictions are said to work for us a weight of glory. Glory is promised to the sufferer for righteousness' sake; and "it is a righteous thing with God, to give rest to them who on such an account are troubled," (2 Thessalonians 1:7). By trouble they are made fit for rest; and the greater the tribulation, the glory, it is likely, will be the greater, to be sure the more welcome. When we look around us and see nothing but matter of grief and sorrow, it will make us look upward to those mansions on high, and long to be there, where sin and suffering will come to a perpetual end. In heaven there will be an eternal calmness and serenity; no sons of violence will be there to disturb the saints in their praises; no enemies will be permitted to roar in that congregation; no fear of prison or any other punishment will be there; but their joy will be like a full sea, and not ebb anymore forever.

APPLICATION

I have now come to the application:

Use 1. If he that will be a saint shall be a sufferer, learn from this, they are far from being saints, who resolve to give out once it comes to suffering. Those are not worthy of the name of disciples, who, like the swallow, will tarry with Christ all the summer, but when the cold and stormy winter approaches, use their wings and leave him. Our Lord says, "He that loves father or mother, or life itself more than me, is not worthy of me:" that is, he is not fit to make you to be offended, and go away from Christ, it is a sign that you prefer ease and peace and prosperity before him, and consequently that you do not have the unfeigned faith of God's elect. If you did indeed believe, Christ would be precious, and that even then, when he is a stone of stumbling, and a rock of offense to others, (1 Peter 2:7). If you did indeed believe, you would be of the apostle's mind, who counted all things as dung, when compared to Christ; and esteeming them to be dung, no wonder if he contentedly suffered the loss of them that his interest in the Lord might be secured, "For whom I have suffered the loss of all things, and do count them but dung that I may win Christ," (Philippians 3:8).

Use 2. If he that will be a saint shall be a sufferer, then it is only reasonable for every saint to expect suffering. Reckon on it that troubles will be met with on your way to heaven; none ever arrived to that fair haven, without being tossed by some tempests. He that goes to sea is not so foolish as to think it will be a perpetual calm during his entire voyage. He that lists himself as a soldier expects some time or another to be engaged. So Christians should sit down, and "count the cost," (Luke 14) before he embarks with Christ, before he lists himself under this Captain of salvation. And certainly it will cost some trouble to be Christ's follower; none ever faithfully served him whose flesh smarted for it; though it must also be affirmed, that this smart of the outward is usually sweetened with a far greater pleasure in the inner man. Our Lord speaks to his disciples plainly, and without a parable. "In the world ye shall have tribulation," (John 16:33); but that their hearts might not be troubled, he tells them first, "In me ye shall have peace." And he adds secondly, "Be of good cheer, I have overcome the world."

Use 3. If he that will be a saint shall be a sufferer, then it is the saint's wisdom to prepare for suffering. Evil days will come, but God has provided armor of proof, which, if you put it on, you shall be able to withstand in the evil day, and having done all to stand. I might here enlarge in going over the Christian's armor, but I shall only single out some pieces, which you must not fail to get and use in a day of suffering, and which, if used skillfully, no force, either of evil men or of angels, shall prevail against you. Though no part of the armor of God is needless, yet especially you must take the shield of faith, the breastplate of love, the helmet of hope, and cry by prayer for continual help and support from above.

1. That you may be armed against sufferings, take to yourself the shield of faith. You are in a battle, men and devils thrusting sore at you that you may fall; what shift can you make without a shield? The shield is armor to the other armor. If faith is strong, your other graces will have the greater vigor, and you stand in the greater stead. Faith will make you victorious. "This is the victory," says the apostle, "that overcometh the world, even our faith," (1 John 5:4). And it may truly be said, "This is also the victory that overcomes the god of this world, even our faith;" faith prevails against both. By faith the worthies of old of whom the world was unworthy, went through all their trials, and yet these trials were very sore. "They were cruelly mocked and scourged, they were stoned, they were sawn asunder, were tempted, were slain with the sword, they wandered about in sheep skins and goat skins, being destitute, afflicted, tormented," (Hebrews 11:37). It is remarkable that the Holy Spirit in describing their punishments says, "They were tempted." It is likely that fair means were used as well as foul, promises of preferment, as

well as threatenings of torment, to draw them away from their integrity; and this was a sore temptation. But faith kept them steadfast, and rendered the temptation ineffectual.

Faith looks to its Author and Finisher, the Lord Jesus, and sees the world vanquished by him, and the principalities and powers of darkness spoiled by him; and therefore concludes that it will not be very long more than a conquest through him that has loved the believer, and this will be obtained. And in the meanwhile, faith relies on the word of promise, and stays the soul on the Lord Jehovah. whereupon the soul is both supported by an everlasting arm, and also kept in perfect peace. "Thou wilt keep him in perfect peace, whose mind is stayed on thee, because he trusteth in thee. Trust ye in the Lord forever, for in the Lord Jehovah is everlasting strength," (Isaiah 26:3-4).

2. That you may be armed against sufferings, put on the breastplate of love. It you love much, you will consent, when called, to suffer much, and will not think much of what you suffer. If your love to the Lord Jesus is as it ought to be, transcendent and flaming, "many waters will not have power to quench it, all the floods that lift up their waves will not be able to drown it," (Song of Solomon 8:7).

Let your love to Christ be surely grounded. Be well acquainted with your lost estate, your absolute need of this Savior, without whom no shift can be made, but wrath and ruin are unavoidable. Be well acquainted with Christ's matchless excellence, and how he is admirably and in every way suited to your desires and necessities, being a prophet to instruct and reduce the ignorant and erring soul, a priest to reconcile his Father to the guilty, a King to rescue and defend from all sorts, even the worst of enemies. And as he is able, so likewise he is ready to do all this, and that for any who desire that all this may be done for them. Indeed he rejects those who like only his priesthood, but count his kingdom to be a hard word, and his commandments to be grievous; but he never denied his benefits to any that were willing to have them all without exception, purity as well as pardon and peace, grace as well as glory.

Our Lord is not unwilling that you should take a view of him. He does not desire to be loved, unless your eyes are enlightened and you see sufficient reason. Sin is loved on a mistake; and it is on a mistake that Christ is despised. If sin were understood, it would be abhorred. and if Christ's worth was weighed and rightly judged of, as he deserves to be, so he would actually be the desire of all nations, as the prophet calls him, (Haggai 2:7).Therefore, know him and let your love spring from a right understanding of him, and then nothing will be esteemed too good or dear to cast away, that you may hold him fast. The world's store is nothing comparable to the benefits, which he has purchased with the price of his blood.

And the most severe laws and edicts of men, the greatest torments that they can invent or inflict, are nothing nearly so dreadful as that *Anathema Maranatha*, which is thundered out against "any man that loves not the Lord Jesus," (1 Corinthians 16:22). *Anathema Maranatha*, signifies, *Let him be accursed until the Lord comes.* Those that do not love Christ will have a curse lying on them that never shall be removed, and that is infinitely worse than any present suffering.

3. That you may be armed against suffering, do not let the helmet of hope be wanting. Your heads may be lifted up with boldness when you have this helmet on. A lively hope will have a great influence to keep your hearts from sinking into despondency. *Hope is styled the anchor of the soul, both sure and steadfast, and entering within the veil,* (Hebrews 6:19). In the storm of trouble, believers should cast anchor, and their anchor must be cast upward; there is the Rock of Ages, and in him the anchor is to be fastened. The ship does not fail while the anchor is cast. But a Christian differs, his anchor is fastened, and yet he fails at the same time; which shows that he fails most safely in the midst of the greatest fluctuations, towards the harbor of peace. Let hope be strong. Hope of a happy conclusion will make present affliction be endured with patience.

It is the business of hope to wait for and expect the accomplishment of the promises. *Fide*, says Luther, *intuetur verbum rei, Spes rem verbi. (Faith beholding the Word's intention is the main property of hope.).* And since the salvation on which hope expects, is so certain, so just at the door, and so exceedingly glorious, hardship and labor in the way to such a rest, may be better dispensed with. When the flesh complains through weakness, and is ready to fail, then hope encourages the heart, and says, "Yet a little while, and he that shall come, will come, and will not tarry;" I expect him, and deliverance and a reward with him, and this expectation of "hope will never make ashamed," (Romans 5:5). This helmet of hope is of singular use. It covers the head of a Christian in the day of battle, it wards off the blows of discouragement, which would strike the head under water. For this reason the apostle is so earnest that the believing Romans, "might be made to abound in hope, through the power of the Holy Spirit," (Romans 15:13).

4. That you may be armed against suffering, cry by prayer for continual help and support from above. Though you are never so completely armed, yet there is need of prayer, to call in fresh and renewed auxiliary force from heaven. Therefore the apostle adds, "Praying always with all prayer and supplication in the Spirit, and watching thereunto with all perseverance," (Ephesians 6:18). When men and devils are wrestling with you, do you wrestle with God; and if you can

only imitate your father Israel, and as princes prevail with God; if you have power with the Almighty, who then can be too strong, too hard for you?

Fill your mouths with arguments, and cry to the Lord, "That since he has led you into the field, he would not leave you in the battle; that since trouble is near, he would not be far off, but near to help you; that since it is for his sake you are persecuted, by his power of providence you may be preserved, and your troubles turned to his honor and your advantage. Tell him that your enemies are his, and it is because you do not dare to displease him that men are enraged against you. Tell him that it is time for him to work, for men have made his law void. Tell him that you look and long for his salvation, and that you will never cease your importunity, until he appears and owns that truth and cause which men endeavor to bear down, but you are standing up for to the death." Prayer has a mighty prevalence. Luther said, there was a kind of omnipotence in this. This weapon has made the church terrible as an army with banners. Persecutors and devils likewise, have many times been worsened by prayer.

Use 4. If he that will be a saint shall be a sufferer, let me exhort and persuade you that are saints, to bear sufferings as become you. Do not let fretting or fear, or sorrow prevail to your discomposure; but manifest to all the world, that you have something of God in you, by undergoing what bare nature would sink under. Suffer not as willful, but as conscientious; be able to give Scripture reasons for what you practice, and for what you refuse. Beg of the Lord to make your way plain; and the way of duty being shown, though there is a lion, or a thorn hedge in the way, go forward notwithstanding.

ENCOURAGEMENTS

And among others, let these encouraging arguments be pondered by you.

1. God is glorified by your sufferings. Indeed, on your adversaries part he is evil spoken of, but on your part he is glorified. It is a sign that you really believe the Lord's greatness and power, when you had rather have the whole world as your enemy, than for him to be your enemy. It is a sign that you indeed believe his goodness and his promises, when you had rather part with all visible comforts, than be cast away from his presence and favor. And by thus believing, you glorify him exceedingly. It argues also that the Lord has your hearts in good earnest, when no troubles, no afflictions, which for his sake you are assaulted with, can alienate your affections from him. Further, you proclaim to all, what a good Master you serve, when your adversaries are not able to divert

you from following him and cannot compel you to forsake his service by all that they do. And who knows what convictions in the consciences of those that observe you may be the effect of your constancy? Who knows that by this means, some may be brought to make trial of your Lord, and so to the liking and loving of him?

2. By your suffering the Gospel is advanced. The mighty power and efficacy of the Gospel is shown forth when it makes and keeps the disciple's hearts undaunted, though sufferings in the most fearful shapes and forms are objected to their view. How is the Gospel magnified, when believers are content to be the mark for an adulterous generation to shoot at, rather than be ashamed of it? It is evident that the Gospel is from God, or else it could not thus support and comfort. The apostle tells the Philippians that his bonds and confinement were to the "Gospel's furtherance," (Philippians 1:12) and enlargement; his brethren grew bold to speak the word without fear, and the word spoken was the more readily entertained, being credited by sustaining Paul and other saints in all their tribulation.

3. By your sufferings, you yourself are dignified. You are highly graced, when called forth to be the Lord's witnesses; the Spirit of glory, and of God rest on you. The Lord singles you out to combat with the powers of earth and darkness, and he will encourage, help, and give you victory. The apostles,

when they were beaten, did not murmur, "but rejoiced that they were counted worthy to suffer shame for the name of Jesus," (Acts 5:41). Shame is dignity, reproach is glory, loss is gain, sorrow is joy, pain is pleasure, when endured for the sake of Christ. Several of the martyrs in the Marian persecution, when they went to the stake, gave thanks on this very account, that they die a death so noble as to die martyrs for the truth against Babel's abominations, and to ascend, as it were, in fiery chariots to the New Jerusalem.

4. When you are suffering, what a stock of prayers is going to you. It is a happiness to be hardly dealt with, so we are praying up harder for. Our tribulation makes the bowels of mercy which are in our brethren to yearn towards us; they are bound with us in the same bonds, and sympathize in our sufferings; this makes them the more instant and earnest with the Father of mercies on our behalf. When James the brother of John had lost his life, being killed by the sword; and Peter had lost his liberty, being apprehended and put in prison, it is said that "prayer was made without ceasing of the church to God for him," (Acts 12:5). And prayer having entered into heaven, brought an angel to his rescue, it shook the chains off Peter's hands, and caused an iron gate of its own accord to open to him. Behold the strength of believer's prayers!

For my own particular, I seriously profess that my imprisonment as most happily in this regard befallen me; I have no reason to be vexed with, but rather to thank my adversaries for their kindness in thus confining of me. The strictness and closeness of my prison has made my case somewhat peculiar; and that also is turned to good, for hereby the spirits of hundreds, both in city and country, were stirred up to pray for me with great fervency and enlargement. And to have so many prayers poured out for one particular person, is an inestimable privilege. My friends, I thank you, God has answered your requests, I have had that in prison, which is ten thousand times better than liberty, than the world, than life, than ten thousand worlds and lives. My enemies, I cannot help but thank you too, because you were the occasion of the mercies I have received; though I really grieve to think that you did me good with so much harm to yourselves.

5. When you suffer, the Lord himself suffers with you. Not only your fellow members, but your Head sympathizes and feels your burdens. "In all your afflictions, he is afflicted," (Isaiah 63:9). You do not have a High Priest that cannot be touched with the feeling of your infirmities. And the effect of this sympathy must needs be a most tender regard to you, and readiness to relieve you in due season. Luther very well observes, that when any member of the natural body is harmed, the sense of pain appears in the head and face, the brows are knit, the forehead wrinkled, and the tongue cries, Oh! The whole countenance is altered. And in like manner it is

49

in the mystical body, when any member is wronged, if the injurious wretches could only see the face of Christ the Head, they might plainly perceive that he feels the stroke, and is wounded in the wounds of his faithful followers. Therefore when Paul, while a zealous son of the Jewish church, persecuted the disciples of the Lord, and being exceedingly mad against them, hailed men and women, and committed them to prison, Christ out of heaven cries out to him, "Saul, Saul, why persecutes thou me?" And since the great Physician is himself wounded in your wounds, you may confidently expect a healing balm from him.

6. To encourage you, consider that the power that rests on you in your sufferings is great. Such a power as shall not only make you as strong as David, but as the angels of the Lord. A saint strengthened by the hands of the mighty God of Jacob, though shot at by the archers, his bow shall abide in strength; therefore in Scripture he is compared to "an iron pillar, to a brazen wall, to a defensed city," (Jeremiah 1:18). To show, that though he is assaulted, and that with violence, yet he stands firm and unmoved. Little do the ungodly think who is the saint's helper. The apostle, considering the sufficiency of that grace which is promised in the evil day, professes that he was not sorry for the day's approach, no so far from that, he glories and takes pleasure in it. "And he said unto me; my grace is sufficient for thee, for my strength is made perfect in

weakness. Most gladly therefore will I rather glory in mine infirmities, that the power of Christ may rest on me. Therefore I take pleasure in infirmities, in reproaches, in necessities, in persecutions, and in distresses for Christ. for when I am weak, then am I strong," (2 Corinthians 12:9-10).

7. The peace that is vouchsafed to sufferers is great. Christ speaks of this peace, and having left this legacy, he adds with reason, that they should not fear or be troubled. "Peace I leave with you, my peace I give unto you; not as the world giveth, give I unto you. Let not your heart be troubled, neither let it be afraid," (John 14:27). How many doubts and fears have been cured by tribulation? When for the Gospel's sake has been submitted to, the heart which before trembled, and was disconsolate, is filled with joy and peace in believing. And indeed, as trouble is an evident token of perdition to the troublers, so to those that for well-doing "are troubled, it is a token of salvation, and that of God," (Philippians 1:28). O the songs that have been sung in the night of distress! O the sweet refreshing visits that the Lord of glory has given to his prisoners; so that those places of confinement, have been sometimes turned into the very suburbs of the New Jerusalem. And do not let the greatness of suffering dismay any; these will only occasion your fuller joy, and more abundant consolation. "For the sufferings of Christ abound in us, so our consolation also aboundeth by Christ," (2 Corinthians 1:5).

8. "If you suffer with Christ, you shall also reign with him," (2 Timothy 2:12). And truly the cross is as light as a feather, if compared with the crown. Send forth your faith as a spy to the heavenly Canaan; let it take a view of the glory there; let it bring only a leaf of the palms that are to be put into your hands, but a gem of the crowns that shortly will be put on your heads, and you will presently be of the apostle's judgment, when he said, "I reckon that the sufferings of this present time, are not worthy to be compared to the glory that shall be revealed in us," (Romans 8:18). Sufferers will find a more abundant entrance into the kingdom. They are with a great deal of honor pointed at. "These are they which came out of great tribulation, and have washed their robes, and made them white in the blood of the Lamb," (Revelation 7:14). How many encouragements are here to suffer; sufficient, if duly weighed, to make you suffer, not only with patience, but with gladness.

Use 5. I shall conclude this doctrine with a caution to the unholy. Do not think your condition to be happy because you are freed from sufferings now. Your sin at last will find you out; it is pursuing after you to overthrow you, and it will, if you do not repent speedily, overtake you. And though you are not in trouble, like other men, that cleanse their hearts, and wash their hands in innocence, eternity will be long enough for you to be plagued, and (woe, woe to you) then your sufferings will be extreme, being not at all sweetened with the least mixture of consolation.

THE SECOND DOCTRINE

The second doctrine is that no sufferings should cause the saints to be afraid.

The text says, "Fear none of those things which thou shalt suffer." Also see. "Strengthen the weak hands, confirm the feeble knees; say to them that are of a fearful heart, be strong, fear not," (Isaiah 37:3-4).

Two things are to be done in the opening of this doctrine. One is to show that there is an aptness in the saints to be afraid of sufferings. The other is to demonstrate the unreasonableness of giving way to this fear.

In the first place I am to show that there is an aptness in the saints to give way to fear, when sufferings are coming. this is implied in the text, "Fear not," which intimates that by fears they would be assaulted, though those fears ought to be repelled. There is a twofold fear; a fear that is a duty, and a fear that is an infirmity.

1. A fear that is a duty, and that is the fear of the Lord. This fear is the beginning of wisdom, and a great preservative from evil; this fear is a grace to be prayed for, and as a grace is promised in the new covenant. "I will put my fear into their

hearts, and they shall not depart from me," (Jeremiah 32:40). This fear has nothing of torment in it; but as it argues the man blessed in whom it has place, so it is very consistent with delight, and great delight. "Blessed is everyone that feareth the Lord, that delighteth greatly in his commandments," (Psalm 112:1). This fear of God will swallow up other fear. If we sanctify the Lord of Hosts in our hearts, by making him our fear and dread, nothing besides will be sufficient to dismay us.

2. There is a fear which is an infirmity, and that is the fear of man, or any evils that on the account of religion may be brought on us. This fear in the text is forbidden. Yet this fear is apt to seize on believers; and truly they find it much more difficult to overcome those fears, than the evils themselves, by which their fears are raised.

There are several things by which fears are apt to be raised in believers.

1. The greatness of the evils which they may be exposed to. Not only their credit, but their livelihood; not only their livelihood, but their lives may be struck at. And running the hazard of losing all, makes timorous nature to advise, and endeavor to dissuade them from it. Our Lord does not limit his followers to venture so far, and no further, but commands expressly to stick at nothing; the nearest relations, the dearest enjoyments must be hated, when they stand in competition with him, that is, less loved than he is; "If any man come to me,

and hate not his father, and mother, and wife, and children, and brethren, and sisters, yea and his own life also, he cannot be my disciple," (Luke 14:26). In times of trouble, men and devils are let more loose, and so are likely to lay hold on Christ's disciples; and the apprehension of such heavy burdens may cause some dismay of spirit.

2. Fear is apt to be raised by the proximity and nearness of evils. When the saints behold their persecutors full of fury, their tongues whet like a sword, and their hands lifted up to give the blow; when they see calamity hastening towards them, and distress like an armed man, which they cannot resist nor avoid, then also their temptation will be strong to fear.

3. These evils are heightened by Satan, who endeavors what he can to impress fear on them. He represents their approaching sufferings, in the most amazing forms, to their imaginations. He tells them that it will be sad to be the scorn of all that look on them, to be counted the filth of the world, and the off-scouring of all things. Satan tells them that it will be sad to have their goods spoiled, their houses taken from them, or leveled with the ground, to see their families undone, and pined with extremity of poverty, to feel in their own persons the hand of violence, especially when sinful compliance may prevent it. The devil buzzes in their ears nothing but dungeons, shackles, swords, axes, faggots, stakes,

furious flames, and in this way endeavors to frighten them out of the way of righteousness.

And it is not unusual when such dreadful things are represented to their imaginations, to assault their faith, and to pester them with unbelieving and blasphemous injections against Christ and his word, endeavoring to make them question the certainty and truth of that glorious "life and immortality which is brought to light by the Gospel," (2 Timothy 1:10). And if these thoughts of infidelity are not watched and prayed against, they will deaden and overwhelm the heart, and prove of a very sinking nature. The Lord therefore is to be entreated to rebuke Satan, who by such blasphemies strikes at his honor, as well as at our safety and peace.

4. Add also, that grace in believers is imperfect, and therefore fear is the more incident. There is much of corrupted, as well as renewed nature; and corrupted nature sides with Satan to frighten them, so that they may cast faith and a good conscience overboard, to keep the vessel from drowning, and secure themselves.

UNREASONABLE FEAR

In the second place, I am to show the unreasonableness of this fear in the saints. Now the unreasonableness of it will be abundantly evidenced by these arguments:

1. Let us compare the mightiest enemies of the saints with him who is their helper. Their adversaries may be mighty, but their helper is Almighty. If the everlasting strength of the Lord Jehovah was only considered, fear would be ashamed of itself in those that belong to him, and are protected by him. Believer's enemies (take the very proudest and strongest of them) in comparison of God are but "Nothing, less than nothing, and vanity," (Isaiah 40). And is it not unreasonable to be afraid of nothing and more unreasonable to be afraid of less than nothing? O you saints, remember what a power is for you; whose hands uphold you, even the very same that upholds all things. Your enemies themselves are in God's hands, they cannot live or move, or act without him; they are only weapons in his hand, which cannot strike one blow more than he sees needful to be given to you; all the wounds which they make shall be healing; and by all their instruments of death they shall only push you forward, and hasten you along in heaven's way.

And if your mighty God rebukes these persecutors, presently they must stoop and bow, and fall down before him. He can tie their hands, nay take away their breath whenever he decides; and when their breath goes forth, and they return to their dust, all their thoughts and designs against you will perish, their envy and revenge will have come to an end, once the vengeance of God, which is the vengeance of hellfire, has taken hold of them. The grave and hell will keep them far from ever molesting you anymore.

2. Let a comparison be made between the craftiness of believer's enemies, and their God's wisdom. The Lord knows the thoughts of man, that they are vanity. He sees their projects, and knows how to frustrate their designs. That is a more notable place, "He disappointeth the devices of the crafty, so that their hands cannot perform their enterprise; he taketh the wise in their own craftiness, and the counsel of the forward is carried headlong," (Job 5:12). The Lord is wise enough, not only to deliver us, but also to take the politicians in their own craftiness. He looks and laughs at the plots of Rome and hell to undermine his kingdom; and that which they intend as a support to the principality of darkness, shall provide its downfall, and Zion shall be built on Babylon's ruins. Solomon says, "there is no wisdom, nor understanding, nor counsel against the Lord," (Proverbs 21:30). And by very good consequence, there is no wisdom, nor understanding, nor counsel against his people; why then should his people fear? "If one wise man were able to defend a little city, having few men in it, against a great King that came against it, and besieged it," (Ecclesiastes 9:14-15).

3. Again, compare the hatred of the saint's enemies with the love, which the lord bears them. Great is the hatred of the

world, greater is the hatred of the devil; but O by infinite degrees greater than either, than both, is the love of God. The love of God to believers is very tender, draws out his care towards them; it is a love that is unchangeable, and so vast as passes all dimensions, and understanding. Therefore, they may be emboldened, and conclude, that this love will be ten thousand times more beneficial than the hatred of any creature can possibly be injurious. In the lovingkindness of God, there is a very great security. "For thou Lord wilt bless the righteous, with favor wilt thou compass him as with a shield," (Psalm 5:12). Our enemies indeed may be many, and may hate us with cruel hatred; but their hatred can no more equal the love of God, than their strength can *vie* with his most glorious power.

4. To show the unreasonableness of the saint's fear, let this be considered: that this God, whose power and wisdom and love are so beyond compare, is ever with them. "Fear thou not," says God by the prophet, "for I am with thee," (Isaiah 4:10). He is not out of the way when his people want him; he is a present help in the time of need. The saints need not go far to seek their God; he fills the earth as well as heaven, and is always ready to show himself strong on behalf of those that trust in him. The Lord is always within hearing; "his eye is on the righteous, and his ear is open to their cry," (Psalm 34:15). He besets his people behind and before, and lays his hand on

them. surely their faith may conclude, since God is so near them, and does beset and fence them, that they are in safeguard.

5. The Lord has engaged by an everlasting covenant to be their God. What, or why therefore should believers fear? "Be not dismayed, for I am thy God," in that fore cited place, (Isaiah 4:10). The Lord stands nearly related to the saints. now it is certain that relation, though it is *minima entitatis*, yet it is *efficia maximam*, it has small entity, but great efficacy. He is their God, their Father, and their Husband; and will he not be a buckler and a fortress to his children, his Son's espoused ones? Will he not take care of his jewels, of his portion, of his peculiar treasure? Well he patiently suffers the apple of his eye to be touched? Let the covenant be studied, and what is implied in that, "I will be to them a God, and they shall be to me a people;" and fear will quickly give way to confidence.

6. The Lord intends to glorify himself in his people's preservation. They need not fear, for God will not miss of his glory; he will be exalted, and therefore his people shall be remembered. God's honor and the saint's safety are twisted together. It was a strong argument which Joshua pleaded; "If Israel fly, and the Canaanites prevail, then what wilt thou do for thy great Name?" (Joshua 7:9). The place in the proverbs, "The name of the Lord is a strong tower, the righteous fly unto it and are safe," may not only thus be expounded, that the

power and faithfulness and mercy of God, by which he has made himself known as by his name, are a safe shelter to the righteous; but also thus the place may be applied. God for his Namesake will be a strong tower to his children; and when they plead his Name, he will glorify himself in their protection. To secure his own honor, he will secure those whom he has taken the charge of; they shall be saved, either *sub coeld*, or *in coelo*; they shall either on earth find a chamber in the day of calamity, until the indignation has passed; or they shall be housed in the celestial mansions, beyond the fear or possibility of danger.

APPLICATION OF THE SECOND DOCTRINE

So, I have demonstrated the unreasonableness of the saint's fear. The application of the doctrine *follows:*

Use 1. Although I would have you to be fearless of suffering, yet some cautions are very needful to be given to you. Rashness is not a grace, though Christian fortitude and courage is.

1. Take heed of augmenting your sufferings needlessly by want of wisdom. Did Abner die as a fool dies? Do believers suffer as fools suffer? When Christ tells his disciples that he sent them forth as sheep among wolves, He bids them to "be

wise as serpents, to beware of men," and uses much of the same language that one of his prophets used before, "Take ye heed everyone of his neighbor, trust ye not in any brother, for every brother will utterly supplant, and every neighbor will walk with slanders, and they will deceive everyone his neighbor, and will not speak the truth; they have taught their tongue to speak lies, and they weary themselves to commit iniquity," (Jeremiah 9:4-5). Be wary what and to whom you speak. In evil times, the prudent keep silence; when men are made offenders for a word. Do not presently credit every professor; there are many false brethren, who though they speak to you in a fair manner, have seven abominations in their heart. Beg wisdom of God that he would guide you with his eye.

But do not let a wily and selfish heart impose on you, and call cowardice by the name of discretion. If your heart is assured to the world, and you are loathe to part with your enjoyments that are earthly, for the enjoyment of Christ and glory; if you look on earthly things as suitable, and spiritual things with a strange eye. suspect that your wisdom does not come from above, and that it will be found as folly in the end.

2. Take heed of suffering as an evil doer. You may in all likelihood have much evil spoken against you, but if it is falsely spoken, it is well enough. That counsel and caution of the apostle, is much to be observed, "But let none of you suffer

as a murderer, or as a thief, or as a busybody in other men's matters," (1 Peter 4:15). You must indeed expect to go through evil report, as well as good, and dishonor as well as honor, (2 Corinthians 6:8). But do not, by sinister aims, by any unwarrantable practice, give conscience just cause to reproach you, as well as your enemies. If you are convinced and suffer as evil doers, if covetousness, lying, injustice, sedition, and rebellion are justly laid to your charge, you will not suffer alone, but the Gospel, and your brethren who are innocent, will be branded for your sakes. O let there be nothing of a crime in your suffering; purely let it be for the sake of purity in worship, and purity of life; then the greater comfort will redound to you, and advantage to the Church of Christ.

3. Take heed of vain glory in your sufferings. That glory is vain and is not worth seeking, much less suffering to attain it. Though a sufferer is in a low condition, yet he is in great danger of being put up with pride. If you design the advancing of your own esteem, and desire to be pointed at as those that are resolute and constant, you are self's, and not Christ's martyrs. How far may pride and vain glory carry an unsound professor? "He may give all his goods to feed the poor," no "his body to be burned," and yet in all this seek himself; and be destitute of love to Jesus Christ, (1 Corinthians 13:3). As the apostle says, "Let nothing be done," (Philippians 2:3) so may I

say, let nothing be suffered "through strife or vain glory." It is a poor thing to be admired and commended of men, if the Lord does not commend you. If you do not seek his approbation, and that honor which comes from him, you may suffer here and eternally besides. Therefore, do not aim at applause, or any such carnal, by, and base end. but let this be your design, that "Christ may be magnified by you, whether by life or by death," (Philippians 1:20).

4. Take heed of being saints in show, and suffering in a good cause with an evil conscience. Hypocritical professors are in a very bad case, because professors are hated by the world; because hypocrites are hated by the Lord. They have a form of godliness, therefore the world strikes at them; they deny the power of godliness, therefore God will not secure them. O therefore beg for upright hearts, and be sure to walk in truth. Do not cover and lust that you judge to be pleasing or profitable with the veil of hypocrisy; but be Jews inwardly, Israelites indeed, not contenting yourselves with a name that you are alive; you may have this, and yet be dead in sin, and at last be damned for it.

Use 2. Let me dissuade you from fearing anything that may befall you for following the Lord Jesus. And let these two things be thought on, that fear is both a torment, and a snare.

1. Fear is a torment. The fearful heart is moved, as the leaves are with the wind. What anguish seizes on the

timorous spirit at the report of evil tidings? How does it sink into a hopeless kind of dejection and so is made more bare and naked to the stroke and dint of calamities which are invading?

2. "Fear is a snare," (Proverbs 29:25). One that fears an arm of flesh will soon be hurried away from God, and into almost any unlawful courses, which by his carnal and disturbed mind are judged to have a tendency to his preservation. Peter fears, and denies Christ, and not only so, but falls accursing; swearing that he did not know him. How is he foiled through fear, who before said, "Though all are offended and forsake thee, yet will not I." Cranmer fears, and against his conscience subscribes to popery; and anathemizes the heresy of Luther and Zwingli, those restorers of the Gospel, and of pure and undefiled religion, which had a long time laid buried by the prevailing of antichrist. Spira fears the losing of his estate, the beggaring of his wife and children, the hazarding of his life, and renounces the protestant religion, but presently was seized on by the pangs of despair; and to the terror and astonishment of all about him, spoke as if he had been in hell itself, even while he was alive. O therefore *be afraid of being afraid*; if this passion prevails, you may quickly fall so foully, as to make you weep bitterly, if not eternally.

ANTIDOTES AGAINST FEAR OF SUFFERING

Use 3. I shall conclude with several antidotes against this sinful and ensnaring fear of suffering. The antidotes are *these:*

1. One antidote is a well-grounded assurance of the love of God. By this love, fear will be cast out. The apostle was so far from being afraid, "that he gloried in tribulation," and the reason was, "because the love of God," that is, the sense and persuasion of it, "was shed abroad in his heart by the Holy Spirit which was given to him," (Romans 5:3,5). When we know that God is ours, we may conclude that afflictions, troubles, and death are ours, that evil men and evil angels too are ours, that is, working out our good, though contrary to their intentions. The enemies of believers are but as so many scullions to scour them, and make them look the brighter. The assured Christian concludes that "greater is he that is in him, than he that is in the world," and therefore he is undaunted. Hark, how confidently the saints of old spoke, who knew the God of Jacob was theirs, and that he was with them. "God is our refuge and strength, a very present help in trouble; therefore will we not fear, though the earth be removed, though the mountains be carried into the midst of the seas," (Psalm 46:1-2).

Therefore give diligence to make your calling and

election sure; bring your grace to the touchstone of the Scripture, that the truth of it may be evident; pray that the Lord world search you, and lead you out of every evil way; and that his Spirit may bear witness with your spirits that you are indeed his children.

2. A second antidote against fear is a clear conscience. A pacified and purified conscience will make the heart very courageous. The heathen poet could say, *Hic murns abeneus esto; Nil conscire sibi, nulla pallescere culpa. Horat. Epistle 2.*

A brazen wall is not a greater security than an unspotted conscience. And Solomon tells us, that a righteous man is bold as a lion. The apostle Paul, when he was pressed out of measure by the weight of troubles, above strength, insomuch that he despaired even of life; was he dismayed? No, so far from that, that he rejoiced. This was strange indeed. What might be the cause of his gladness, when since being judged, his condition was so exceedingly doleful? "Our rejoicing is this, even the testimony of our conscience, that in simplicity, and godly sincerity, not with fleshly wisdom, but by the grace of God we have had our conversation in the world," (2 Corinthians 1:12). Therefore do not make any breach on conscience, especially in troubled times, by closing with temptations, for at that breach, fear will assault you.

3. A third antidote against gear is trusting in God. David says, "What time I am afraid, I will trust in thee," (Psalm

56:3). Fear is the distemper and the remedy against it is faith in God. So, "He shall not be afraid of evil tidings, his heart is fixed," (Psalm 112:7). Pray for the increase of faith. Be well acquainted with the promises, where God has said he will be a shield, a hiding place, a covert, a strong tower, a Savior; and these promises will be as food for your faith to live on, and to grow strong by. But be sure to let your trusting in God be joined "with the doing of good," (Psalm 37:3) with a desire and design to please him; else he will reject your confidence as presumption, and you shall not prosper in it.

4. A fourth antidote against fear is calling on God. David, when he was in danger, cries that he may be led to the Rock that was higher than he; when surrounded with enemies "he gave himself unto prayer," (Psalm 109:4) and by this means he got above his fears and terrors. He tells us how effectual prayer was, "I sought the Lord, and he heard me, and delivered me from all my fears," (Psalm 34:4). The Coneys are a feeble folk, but have their dwelling among the rocks. You may learn a great deal of wisdom from those little creatures. By faith and prayer you should be working yourselves further into the Rock of Ages, and that Rock you will find impregnable.

5. A fifth antidote against fear is a heavenly conversation. Those who are much above, that have their treasure in that place, where neither moth corrupts, nor

thieves approach, will not be afraid of prisons, of being robbed, of being slain for the testimony of Jesus. Their souls cannot be touched, their best riches are durable, and out of their enemies' reach; their adversaries cannot by distraining take away their glory or grace from them. And when this life is done, they will enter on that life which is infinitely better.

Those who walk closely with God, and whose hearts are frequently given to him as a heave-offering, being lifted up in his ways, who everyday take several turns in the city that has foundations; who often think of the glorious prize, and most fully satisfied in the uninterrupted and never ending enjoyment of God; such will be indifferent with what they meet with on earth; they will not be afraid of what man can do, since when their enemies do their worst, they do their best, for when they take away their lives, they only send them to where they long and groan earnestly to be received; and to make their everlasting abode.

The apostle informs us, "That they who mind earthly things are enemies to the cross of Christ," (Philippians 3:18-19). They do not feel its crucifying virtue, they are afraid of it, they are offended at it. but as for himself, "whose conversation was in heaven, and who perpetually from thence was looking for a Savior, the Lord Jesus Christ," he knew how to be abased, how to be hungry, how to suffer need, and learned in whatever state he was therewith to be content, (Philippians

4:11-12 compared with Philippians 3:20).

6. A sixth antidote against fear is a due consideration of who your enemies and troublers are. Bring them into the sanctuary, and there take a view of them, weigh them in the balance, and themselves with all their power, will be found so light that you will conclude it to be a very vain fear, which such vain and weak creatures as they are, raise in you.

1. Your enemies are only men; let them do their worst, their most, they can kill the body. "Cease ye from man," says the prophet, "whose breath is in his nostrils, for wherein is he to be accounted of." The hand of man, as it is not able to support us, so neither to throw us down; and consequently he no more deserves to be feared than to be trusted by us.

2. Your enemies are men whom the Lord hates and sets his face against. He ordains his arrows against the persecutors, (Psalm 7:13). God shall shoot at them, suddenly they shall be wounded. He is more angry at them, than they can be enraged against you; and it will not be long before he eases himself and you of these burdensome oppressors. "Therefore saith the Lord, the Lord of Hosts, the mighty one of Israel, I will ease me of my adversaries, and avenge me of my enemies," (Isaiah 1:24). Fear becomes them that have such a mighty God as their enemy, but not you that have him as your Father and Defender.

THE THIRD DOCTRINE

The third doctrine: among other troubles, some believers endure bonds and imprisonment.

In the catalogue of sufferings, imprisonment is reckoned by the Holy Spirit. "And others had trial of cruel mockings and scourgings, yea moreover of bonds and imprisonment," (Hebrews 11:36). And the apostle speaks after this manner, "And now behold I go bound in the spirit unto Jerusalem, not knowing the things that shall befall me there, save that the Holy Spirit witnesseth in every city, saying that bonds and afflictions abide me," (Acts 20:22-23). The members of Christ, though made free by their Head, yet may have fetters put on them by unreasonable men. In the imprisonment of the saints, two things are to be considered:

1. Their confinement, and the restraint that is laid on them. Liberty is agreeable to nature, it is therefore a great trial to lose it; and the closer the imprisonment is, nature accounts it the more irksome. To have lovers and friends and acquaintances put far away may well be looked on as a great affliction. To be within double doors, and those doubly barred; to look through iron gates, is a condition which needs something from above to sweeten it.

2. Their being numbered among evildoers is another part of the imprisoned believers' trial. As the Lord himself "was

numbered among the transgressors," (Isaiah 53:12) so are his prisoners. The same jail contains thieves, harlots, and the witnesses of Jesus; their innocence is sullied, and things that they do not know are laid to their charge. But the Lord has promised that within a while, "their righteousness shall be brought forth as the lights, and their judgment as the noon day," (Psalm 37:6).

Now the reason why the saints are imprisoned by their enemies is *twofold*:

1. That they may be punished. If their enemies can go no further, they will go so far, and by it they think to take some revenge on them; though they little imagine what a sweet place they send the saints to; God turns their revenge into a kindness.

2. That they may be hindered from doing good is another reason why the saints are confined. They went about doing good while liberty was enjoyed, therefore they are restrained, and their feet made fast, that they may no longer be thus employed, though it is as their Lord and Master himself was in the days of his flesh. But it is the application of this doctrine which I principally intend.

APPLICATION OF THE THIRD DOCTRINE

Use 1. How the saints should behave themselves when they are imprisoned. I shall direct their carriage in these particulars:

1. They must carry themselves humble before God. Sin and the desert of it should be called to remembrance; and how a worse place than a prison has been justly merited. You should lament not improving liberty while you had it, your unprofitableness, your usefulness, that so little good was done, when you had opportunities in your hands. The cross indeed that is laid on you is a badge of honor; and yet with it there is somewhat medicinal in it, which argues remainders of spiritual distempers that should be a matter of humiliation. The more humble and contrite you are, the more visits you are likely to have from the high and lofty One, who inhabits eternity. "He dwells with the lowly, that he may revive the spirit of the humble, and that he may revive the heart of the contrite ones," (Isaiah 57:15).

2. You must carry yourselves meekly and modestly towards your enemies; you must bless them that curse you, and pray for your despiteful persecutors, (Matthew 5:44). Do not call the wildfire of your own passions by the name of zeal. and ever remember that excellent and divine maxim, "The

wrath of man worketh not the righteousness of God," (James 1:20). Imitate the perfect pattern, who when he was reviled, did not revile in return, when he suffered, he did not threaten, but committed himself to him that judges righteously. Meekness and humility will be lovely and convincing too, in the eyes of your adversaries, and they may be brought to acknowledge, if Christ has any followers, you must resemble his followers who are and should be like him.

3. Do not be daunted at imprisonment. Look with another kind of countenance than those do that suffer for evil doing. Do not let your joys be so low as to be in the power of creatures to rob you of them. Show by your cheerfulness that you have chosen that good part which men cannot take away from you. Check your spirits when they begin to despond, and say with David, "Why art thou cast down, O my soul? And why art thou disquieted within me? Hope thou in God, for I shall yet praise him, who is the health of my countenance, and my God," (Psalm 43:5). And that you may be in this way fortified, beg that the Lord would strengthen you according to his glorious power with all might, to all patience and longsuffering with joyfulness, (Colossians 1:11).

4. Since you are taken off from other business, abound more in duty. Now the throne of grace should be often visited; and the Word which strengthens in weakness, which revives in heaviness, should be more than ever searched into. It is fit

that prisons should be houses of prayer. Being sequestered from the world, you should be more with God. Pull up all the flood gates, and let the stream of your affections run with a holy violence towards him. Ever be telling him what you need, what you desire, and be encouraged by the promise that he has made "to satiate the weary, and to replenish every sorrowful soul," (Jeremiah 31:25).

Fellowship with God will make solitude pleasant; you will find, that though you are alone, you have the best company. If you are continually almost speaking to God by supplication and thanksgiving, and hearing what he speaks to you, by his Word and providences and Spirit, you will have reason to profess that a prison is one of the best places of abode, next to the sanctuary and the New Jerusalem.

5. Let imprisonment be improved so as to further your progress in sanctification. Ransack every corner of your hearts. Deal much more severely with your lusts than men can deal with you; cry out with violence against your fleshly and worldly inclinations. It is sin that deadens and imprisons your spirits; the more sanctified you are, the more you will be at liberty. Tell the Lord, and speak it from your very hearts, that sin is the worst of all your adversaries, and that the remainders of the old man are worse than any fetters in the world. Never leave the Lord alone, until you find the body of death pining and dying sensibly away, the world as a

contemptible thing more under your feet, and your inward man increasing strength, and growing up apace to "the measure of the stature of the fullness of Christ," (Ephesians 4:13).

Use 2. Of consolation to imprisoned believers. Several things may be suggested as grounds of comfort and encouragement.

1. God can come to his people through barred and bolted doors. No dungeon can keep the prisoner far from him. We read that the Lord came to his disciples while the door was shut, and said, "Peace be unto you." And if he comes into prison, and the door is shut, and by his Spirit says, "Peace be to thee," the prisoner's heart will leap for joy; he will not say, "How dreadful," but "How delightful is this place? This is no other than the house of God, and this is the gate of heaven." Our adversaries, let them dispose of us where and how they please, for they cannot shut us up from his presence. and where his gracious presence is vouchsafed, there is rest; all inconveniences and miseries are so light that they are hardly worth taking notice of.

2. The heart may be enlarged where the body is confined. The soul may be brought out of prison, when the body is committed to it. In the *form of law* such an idea runs this way, that the jailer takes the body of such a one. Verily they have no power over the spirit. What believer would not

be content to be confined, on condition that his heart might be made more free *to* duty, more free *in* duty? Upon the condition that his desires might swell and overflow, and his longings after the God of all grace, might grow much stronger than the thirst of the most sensual after pleasures, or of the most worldly minded after gold and silver.

3. The Lord who will condemn those that do not visit the prisoners, will not fail to visit them himself, (Matthew 25). And as they need more refreshments, they shall surely enjoy them. He will behold them with a reconciled face, and say to them, "I am your light and your salvation," do not be terrified with the darkness of the calamitous day in which you live. The groaning of the prisoner pierces the heavens, and enters into the ear of the Lord of the Sabbath, who will return and answer of peace and consolation.

4. The prisoners of Christ are prisoners of hope. They are only doing the King of saint's pleasure. If Christ says, "Come forth," even a Lazarus shall break out of a grave. And if he has the key of the grave, surely the keys of prisons are at his command; they cannot hold any whom he has a mind to set at liberty. Prisons may soon grow sick of the saints, and vomit them out as the whale did Jonah. However, it will not be long before the day of glorious liberty, and of full redemption comes; and then the adversaries of the saints will be bound hand and foot, and be thrown into outer darkness; and the

saints will have liberty to enter into the kingdom prepared for them, to see God face to face, without any let from others or themselves, and to live eternally in "his presence, where there is fullness of joy, and pleasures forevermore," (Psalm 16:11).

THE FOURTH DOCTRINE

The fourth doctrine: the devil is the imprisoner of believers.

The text says, "Behold the devil shall cast some of you into prison." The words may be referred more particularly to the ministers, or more generally to the saints in Smyrna.

1. More particularly to the ministers. As by one candlestick the whole body of the congregation, so by one angel, the whole company of the pastors are to be understood. "Unto you I say, and to the rest in Thyatira," (Revelation 2:24). That is, to you, the ministers, and the rest of believers. So here, "The devil shall cast some of you into prison;" that is, you who are the shepherds, that so against the flock he may have the greater advantage.

Faithful ministers cannot and never could be endured by Satan. He endeavors to corrupt them, to puff them up with pride, to draw them aside by filthy lucre, to make them fall some way or another; and he does it with this design, that their doctrine may be the less heeded, and his kingdom may be not so much weakened by them. But if he is not able to corrupt, he will be industrious to discourage them. They trouble him, and will not leave him alone, they will not suffer the strong man armed to keep his house in peace, but by warning, exhorting, reproving, and rebuking the secure and ungodly, endeavor to dispossess him. No wonder that the devil becomes angry at them, and flings them out of their houses into places of confinement.

The prince of darkness wishes that these stars would not shine; he would gladly have these candles put under bushels. For light discovers what Satan is, what a defiled and hating spirit; it discovers what his works are, namely to pollute us, and by polluting to fit us for perdition. Light also discovers what sin is, and the inconceivable needfulness and excellence of the Lord Jesus. And on this the devil's vessels, several of them, are made to bethink themselves, and "are delivered from the power of darkness, and translated into the kingdom of the Son of God," (Colossians 1:13). The joyful sound of man's salvation is harsh in Satan's ears; he therefore imprisons the publishers of these glad tidings, and close sometimes, that the flock may be edified, neither in a public, nor a private way.

2. The words may be referred more generally to the saints in Smyrna. Every member of Christ is hated by the devil, and he would gladly tear them from Him; this roaring

lion would make every sheep his prey; therefore he raises persecution to dishearten them from following their great Shepherd. Though in this the subtle serpent plays the fool egregiously; for the saints grow more acquainted with their Lord in prison, and grow more like him, and are knit closer to him ever after.

But it may be inquired here, how the devil casts the saints into prison. The resolution of this shall be in these three particulars:

1. The devil stirs up false accusers of believers. The Name which the Holy Spirit gives him in the text is διαβόλῳ, a calumniator, or *false accuser*. He accurses the brethren before God, and his instruments at his instigation do it before men. He inspired false witnesses against Christ; he does the same against Christ's followers. This unclean spirit is utterly alienated both from truth and love. He is the father of malicious lies, especially against the brotherhood. Words that they never spoke, even which to speak is against their conscience; deeds that they never did, even which they abhor to do, are notwithstanding fathered on them by the children of the father of lies and liars.

2. The devil cherishes in the minds of his servants, unreasonable jealousies and surmises concerning saints; and this is another matter which occasions their imprisonment; they are looked on as dangerous persons, and that it is

inconvenient and unsafe to have them at liberty. As the primitive Christians had the skins of brute beasts on them, and then were worried. So believers are represented by Satan to the minds of their enemies, as enemies to government, as turners of the world upside down, as those that would set the nation in a combustion. But O how far they are from deserving such a character! They pray earnestly and desire heartily, under authority to live quiet and peaceable lives in all godliness and honesty. They are indeed the disciples of the Prince of peace, and make conscience of following after peace and holiness, without which no man shall see the Lord, (Hebrews 12:14).

3. The devil heightens the enmity against, and hatred of piety, that naturally is in the minds of the ungodly; so that it breaks out into acts of cruelty and injustice. Although corrupted nature of itself is very furious, yet it is more violent when the devil joins with it. He can set an edge on the lusts of men, and make them the more impetuous. When concupiscence is blown up by an unclean spirit, how does it burn and flame then? When pride is heightened by a proud devil, how uncontrollable is it by any advice or consideration? And in like manner, when envy, hatred, and malice, and uncharitableness (as they are put together in the Litany) are made more keen by a spiteful Satan. No wonder if the tongues

of the ungodly prove scourges, and their hands strike at believer's liberty, if not at their lives.

APPLICATION OF THE FOURTH DOCTRINE

Use 1. Of counsel and advice to persecutors. I do not know if this book may find its way into the hands of one of them. Understand O enemy, whoever you are, that you have a friend at the gatehouse who wishes you well, who prays for your welfare as well as his own, who would stop you in your pernicious way; not so much for the saint's sake as for your own. for you do yourself, not them, the greatest mischief. Do not let, O persecutors, your rage stop your ears, be a little in cool blood, and hearken to these two words of counsel:

1. Consider then by whom you are acted. The devil casts the saints into prison, so then whose instruments and servants are you? Is there not a better Master to be served, a better work to be employed about? What thanks do you think our Lord Christ will give you for the service you do to this destroyer.

But you will say, "It is zeal that puts us on what we do, and we hope we do God and his church good service." Yes, so the Jews thought they served God, when they set themselves against his Son. and Christ himself foretold this, "They shall put you out of the synagogues, they shall excommunicate you, yea the time cometh, that whosoever killeth you will think that he doth God good service," (John 16:2).

2. O that you would become friends to yourselves by being friends to the saints. The apostle Paul says that before his conversion, "he was exceedingly mad against the Lord's disciples," (Acts 26:11). He showed himself to be exceedingly mad indeed, to set himself against them that were so dear to the Lord Jesus. But at last he is recovered to his wits, he is cured of that persecuting frenzy that possessed and acted him, and then "he preached that faith, which once he endeavored to destroy," (Galatians 1:23). O that you would become propagators of the Gospel which you now oppose and hinder from being preached.

Use 2. Of consolation to the prisoners of Jesus Christ.

1. Think of how weak the devil is, if compared with the Captain of your salvation. Christ has fought with this old dragon and overcome him, he has tried his strength, and has been much too hard for him. He has taken the devil captive and holds him in a chain. As the great emperor and conqueror Tamerlane kept Bajazet the Turkish king in an iron cage. So the Lord Jesus, having subdued Satan, keeps him in shackles; he cannot stir to destroy a swine, much less to molest a saint without Christ's leave to do anything to his faithful followers that may be truly to their prejudice?

2. There is less danger when Satan rages, than when he

flatters; it is better that he should cast you into prison for well doing, than draw you into his snare, and to the commission of evil. His pleasing temptations are most hard to be resisted. When you see him furious and playing the devil indeed, as it is a sign that he has come after you but possibly lost you to God, so his enmity is being more perceivable by his outward assaults on you, and it will make you fly to that "merciful and faithful High Priest who knows how to succor them that are tempted," (Hebrews 2:18). And besides his hatred at such a time being so visibly discovered, it will make you more sober and vigilant ever after; and to put on the armor, that you may stand against all his wiles and all his devices.

3. The devil may have great wrath, "but he hath but a short time," (Revelation 12:12). He is more busy because he is aware that your warfare will shortly be at an end; and that the spiritual combatants, within a few years will be conquerors and crowned. Happy are those that are above! Devils cannot come at them! They do not know what temptation means. It is no more possible for any of Satan's fiery darts to hit any of the saints in glory, than for an arrow that we shoot upward into the air to hit the sun in the firmament. Now you saints that are below, will come to be above shortly. "Your salvation grows nearer and nearer every day," (Romans 13:11).

The Fifth Doctrine

The fifth doctrine is that saints are imprisoned that they may be tried.

The devil, says the text, shall cast some of you into prison that you may be tried. The word in the original is πειρασθῆτε that you may be tempted. Now trial, or temptation, is sometimes taken in a bad, or sometimes in a good sense, and the text may be understood either way.

1, Trial or temptation may be taken in a bad sense as referred to the devil. Certainly he, by imprisoning believers, designs to make them wear of their Lord's yoke; he would gladly have them murmur and be impatient under restraint, and draw them to some sinful compliance, to the wounding of their consciences for the regaining of their liberty. He endeavors to make them grow discontent, and quarrel at the Lord's dispensations; that their enemies which are vile, and the basest of men, should prosper, and for themselves in the meantime to be exposed to so many hardships and inconveniences notwithstanding the integrity of their hearts, and the unblameableness of their conversations.

2. Trial or temptation may be taken in a good sense, as referred to God's permitting the saints to be thus exercised. He certainly has a wise and gracious and holy end in it. It is true, "God cannot be tempted with evil, neither tempteth he

any man," (James 1:13). And yet it is expressly affirmed that God did tempt Abraham, (Genesis 20:1). How shall these two places be reconciled? I answer, that temptation spoken of by the apostle James, is to be understood concerning "drawing away and enticing to wickedness," (James 1:14). And this God does not tempt; he neither infuses, nor excites any sinful inclinations in the heart of man, but strictly forbids sin, and will severely punish it. Thus men are tempted by Satan, and especially by their own lusts. But that temptation spoken of by Moses, is as much as trying or making proof of Abraham's sincerity. And this to tempt, is not at all unbecoming or inconsistent with the Lord's holiness and goodness. and when he suffers believers to be imprisoned, it is for their trial that he does it.

WHAT ASPECTS OF THE SAINTS ARE TRIED DURING IMPRISONMENT

Now here I shall first show what of the saints is tried by imprisonment, and sufferings of the like nature. Secondly, to what end they are thus tried.

In the first place, what of the saints is tried by imprisonment, and sufferings of like nature. First, their faith, Secondly, their love. Thirdly, their subjection and obedience.

1. Their faith is tried. Those that can lose what they have for Christ, it argues a full persuasion that Christ is better than their earthly enjoyments, and that they believe there is such a fullness in him that can make up all their losses. Such esteem the promise of eternal blessings, exceeding great and precious, who are resolved to embrace them whatever they fling away besides. When in a good cause we lightly esteem liberty and outward accommodations, it shows that we have faith "which is the substance of things hoped for, and the evidence of things not seen," (Hebrews 11:1). Our faith gives a subsistence so, and mightily realizes those things which as yet we have only the hopes of enjoying; and makes the great things of another world evident, though not to be seen or possessed until hereafter. Faith is a noble grace, for it glorifies God exceedingly; when a man on the Lord's word, will consent to quit all that is near and dear to him, in expectation of a kingdom and glory which no man alive ever saw.

2. By imprisonment and other sufferings, the believer's love is tried. Those who can undervalue liberty and livelihood and life for the sake of the Son of God, may boldly say as Peter did in another case, "Lord, thou knowest all things, thou knowest that we love thee," it is manifest that they love the Lord Jesus in sincerity. But if when the world and Christ stand in competition, we hold to the world, and despise the Lord, certainly our love is but a painted fire, and not a real

one. Love is a grace of a uniting nature. The history tells us, "That the soul of Jonathan was knit to David, and he loved him as his own soul;" and we find that the displeasure which Saul had . conceived against David, and the danger that Jonathan was in, for his affection's sake, could not cool, much less quench his love. If we love our Lord, our souls will be knit to him; and troubles will be so far from dissolving the union, that they will cause us to cling closer and clasp the faster about him.

3. By imprisonment and sufferings of the like nature, there is a trial made of the believer's subjection and obedience. When they will do for God, though presently suffering for God; this argues that they have learned to deny their own wills, and taken the Word and will of God as their guide and rule. When they regard the commands of God above the commands of men, are awed by the threats of men, and dread God's displeasure more than a man's anger; this is a demonstration that they have further submitted to Christ's scepter, and that the promise of the covenant is fulfilled. "I will put my laws into their minds, and write them in their hearts, and I will be to them a God, and they shall be to me a people," (Hebrews 8:10).

THE POINT OF IMPRISONMENT

In the second place, I am to tell you what end God will have for his saints who are thus tried.

1. That the truth of their grace may be evident; and great peace must be the concomitant of that evidence. When their gold is tried in the fire, and glistens the more, shines the brighter, they may be pronounced rich indeed. The man that is rich in the world, has no reason to glory in his riches, for he is indeed a beggar in comparison.

2. Those are tried that Satan may be silenced. He can no longer say that the saints are mercenary or selfish, when self is thus denied, when peace of conscience is preferred before the greatest outward peace and prosperity; and so the inheritance above may be secured, they put it to the venture what the world can do for them. The Lord may say to Satan (and this accuser of the brethren may have nothing to comply) "Hast thou considered my suffering servants, how perfect and upright they are? They fear God, and eschew evil, though by departing from evil they make themselves a prey."

3. Believers are tried, that God who upholds them may be honored. The Lord is with them in the furnace; he keeps them like the bush in the midst of the flaming fire, unconsumed. He shows his wisdom and grace, in so tempering the furnace, as that it is both tolerable, and also effectual to their refining. The saints have abundant cause to

readily acknowledge that their support in trouble, their benefit by trouble, and their deliverance out of trouble, is wholly ascribed to God; and he is glorified by this, which is so just an acknowledgment.

APPLICATION OF THE FIFTH DOCTRINE

Use 1. Of admonition to unsound professors. Be restless until you are searched and changed so, as to have truth in your inward parts; else you will never abide the trial. in the time of temptation, your sand foundations will deceive you; "your building will fall, and great will be the fall of it," (Matthew 7:27).

You will fall away further from God, more foully into sin, more deep into hell; and all these falls will be great and dreadful.

1. You that are unsound, in times of trial will fall away further from God. Some of you, though never brought quite home, yet have been almost persuaded, have not been far from the kingdom of heaven. But all this common work, if you rest in it, will die away; when Christ puts you on suffering, you will forsake him. "Suffer" is a hard word, who can bear it? And when you leave the Lord, you bid farewell to the Father of mercies; the God of love, and of all grace, the foundation of living waters, the Prince of peace, the only Savior. Well, may I

cry out, O how much folly there is in backsliding!

2. You will fall more foully into sin. God may quickly throw the reins out of his hands on the neck of corrupted nature; and where may you be carried? Apostatizing professors often turn most profane; they outrun, as to riot and excess, the wretches that never pretended to religion. The conscience that was once awakened, if it falls asleep again, sleeps more soundly. The heart that was once restrained from sin, that restraint being gone, is more eager to commit iniquity than before. No, it is sometimes observed, that backsliding professors even become cruel persecutors of those ways which once were forwardly owned by them. If this is not the unpardonable sin, I am sure it comes to the very brink of it.

3. You will fall more deep into hell at last. Christ tells us that "the last end of such is worse than their beginning," (Matthew 12:45) and that both as to sin, and as to punishment. How large will the vial of wrath be that is to be emptied on the apostate's head? How hot will their place in the lake that burns with fire and brimstone be? Those, that as the apostle speaks "are twice dead, plucked up by the roots," (Jude 12). The second death will be more terrible to them, they will be eternal fuel to a more furious flame. The sufferings of the saints, whether imprisonment or death, are not worthy to be named the same day, with everlasting confinement to outer darkness, and suffering in the highest degree and fullest

measure of eternal damnation. Consider this, you hypocrites that are rotten at heart, that have God in your mouths, but he is far from your reins. O how long will it be before you attain to uprightness!

Use 2. Of encouragement to the saints when they are exercised with trials.

1. The Lord has promised to keep you when you are tried. He may fan and winnow, but not a grain of corn shall fall to the ground so as to be lost. The Scripture is very observable, "Because thou hast kept the word of my patience, I also will keep thee from the hour of temptation, which shall come on all the world, to try them that dwell on the earth," (Revelation 3:10). He will keep from the hour of temptation, that is, from the prevalence of it, and the corruption by temptation in that hour. But then you must be sure to keep his Word, which is called the word of his patience, because it proposes Christ as an example of patience, and lays an injunction on you to be like him. And if you look on this word, as your food, as your medicine, as your treasure, as your armor, as your heritage, I hope you will look on it as well deserving to be kept by you.

2. Your trials will make you to grow rich in grace. Grace is of that nature that it increases and gathers strength by exercise. As the widow's oil by being drawn out multiplied, so grace is augmented, not diminished by being used. Harken to

the apostle, "Knowing that tribulation worth patience," (Romans 5:3-5); not only tries patience, but works patience; "and patience experience, and experience hope, and hope maketh not ashamed." The righteous are not stopped by trials and difficulties as discouraged people, but hold on their way, no not only hold on, but grow and go stronger. "And they that have clean hands shall wax stronger and stronger," (Job 17:9).

3. After you have endured trials, you shall be owned and crowned. "Blessed is the man that endureth temptation, for when he is tried, he shall receive the crown of life, which the Lord hath promised to them that love him," (James 1:12). And that crown when received will make all pains and disgrace and sufferings to be forgotten.

The Sixth Doctrine

The sixth doctrine is that the tribulation of believers will not last always, after ten days, that is, a short time, a period will be put to it.

You shall have tribulation for ten days. The Holy Spirit reckons by days, not years, and according to the usual manner, in Scripture, a certain number is put for an uncertain, ten days for a few days. The apostle calls the troubles of believers not only "light afflictions," but affirms that they are "but for a moment," (2 Corinthians 4:17); and because they are only for a moment, surely they are much lighter.

The arguments to confirm this doctrine are *these:*

1. One shall be drawn from the desire in Christ the Head to have his members with him. Therefore they shall not be long absent from him; and when they are with him, no troubles at all shall be their companions. Christ, in the days of his flesh, prayed thus, "Father I will that those also whom thou hast given me, be with me where I am, that they may behold my glory, which thou hast given me, for thou lovedst me before the foundation of the world," (John 17:24). Christ has now gone to his Father, and he has prepared mansions for the saints, and those mansions shall not be long empty. Believers groan to be clothed on with their house which is from heaven; to be absent from the body, and to be present with the Lord. The Lord Jesus desires and has prayed for their company. Surely it will not be long before those who are so mutually desirous of each other, come together.

2. A second argument shall be drawn from the shortness of the triumph of the saint's adversaries. God will quickly cut asunder the cords of the wicked, that plow on Zion's back, and make their furrows long. "I have seen," says David, "the wicked in great power, and spreading himself like a green bay tree; yet he passed away, and lo he was not, yea I sought him, but he could not be found." His great power, which he abuses

to oppress and trouble, and himself too, shall quickly pass away. All the glory of the ungodly is as a dream, and is chased away as a night vision. And when they are laid in the dust, and death is feeding on them, they can devour the upright no longer. And truly the more violent they are, the shorter oftentimes their triumph is; cruelty ripens them for vengeance.

3. A third argument shall be drawn from the shortness of the saint's continuance in this vale of tears. Their tribulation cannot possibly be of any long duration. They are but travelers through the world, and will quickly be at their journey's end. A few years, no perhaps a few months will bring them to eternity; and when time is no longer there will be no longer trouble. The thoughts of death, though terrible to the ungodly, as putting a full stop to all their consolation, may be refreshing to the saints. Death is their last enemy; after death, no enemy can molest them. Their days are swifter than a weaver's shuttle; they hasten to an end, as the ships of desire to the haven, or the eagle to the prey. And as their days pass away, so their troubles and distresses make speed to a conclusion.

4. A fourth argument shall be drawn from the saint's immediate entrance into rest on their dissolution. The apostle joins "being dissolved" and "being with Christ" together; and speaking of believers in general, he says, "For we know that if

our earthly house of this tabernacle were dissolved, we have (not we shall have, but we have) a building of God, an house not made with hands, eternal in the heavens," (2 Corinthians 5:1). The spirits of just men immediately on their separation, are made perfect, perfectly free from sin and misery, which while united to the body they were loaded with.

The papists distinguish the church into *Triumphantem in caelis, militantem in terra, laberantem in purgatorio, Triumphant in heaven, militant on earth, laboring in purgatory,* the Scripture nowhere mentions, but expressly affirms the contrary, "Blessed are the dead that die in the Lord, from henceforth, yea saith the Spirit, that they may rest from their labors," (Revelation 14:13).

Several miserably deluded souls argue for perfection here; else they say how can the saints be fitted for glory, if they are defiled all their days? It is easily answered, that the work of grace is carried on all their lifetime, and at their dissolution their souls are perfected. Death may be called a great change, not only in regard of the body, but in regard of the soul too, because the soul is perfectly purified, and sin is quite and clean abolished. Neither let it seem absurd that such a change should be; for in the first moment of conversion there is an alteration or change from no grace to grace, surely it is not unreasonable to think that at the moment of dissolution, there should be a change from imperfect grace to grace that is complete. So the penitent thief's soul was perfected at his expiring, else he could not have been with Christ in paradise on the day he died.

It is plain that the saints, on their departure, henceforth enter into rest; therefore it must be granted, that their tribulation is but, as they are, short lived; no perhaps they may outlive their tribulation, and behold a *lightsome eventide* after a day of darkness and gloominess. They may live to see the Gospel esteem, after disgrace, and peace on Israel after trouble.

APPLICATION OF THE SIXTH DOCTRINE

Use 1. Is the tribulation of the saints short? Then let their faith not fail; let it hold out a little longer, and its work will be at an end. Let faith only keep up the ship a little while longer in the storm, and it will be safely landed. Lean a few more days on the promises of support and shelter, and you will be past the pikes, and beyond all peril. When you are entered into the city of God, the door will be shut; and as you shall come out no more, so no evil shall enter after you, to molest or grieve you.

Use 2. Is the tribulation of the saints short? Then let their patience not grow weary. Now patience indeed is a needful grace, but hereafter there will be no necessity or use of it, because you shall never feel any more burdens. The benefit of affliction, and the nearness of your rest, should induce you to bear all with cheerfulness; When you see the purpose of the Lord, you will confess "they are happy that endure," (James 5:11).

Use 3. Is the tribulation of the saints short? Then let their expectation be raised. Yet a little while and he that shall come, will come, and will not tarry, (Hebrews 10:37). Your Lord will be as a hart, or your roe on the mountains of separation; and when he comes, he will wipe away tears from all faces, and for all your affliction and tribulation, you shall have joy and triumph double, triple, even ten thousand times ten thousand.

Use 4. Is the tribulation of the saints short? See the difference between the saints and sinners. The saint's sufferings are like the sinner's ease and prosperity, both for a moment. Do not let the world imagine believers to be miserable; their misery is no longer than this world's happiness. And as the men of the world cannot be counted happy, because their happiness does soon vanish, so neither can believers justly be esteemed miserable, because their misery is so transient. What is it to have tribulation for ten days, and then to triumph in the presence of God, and of the

Lamb forever.

THE SEVENTH DOCTRINE

The seventh doctrine teaches that whatsoever sufferings he is exposed to, a Christian must be faithful.

All the children of Abraham should resemble their father; of whom it is said that the Lord "found his heart faithful before him," (Nehemiah 9:8). This charge in the text is strict, "Be thou faithful:" And truly it is needful, if these three things are considered.

1. A Christian's heart is treacherous, and apt to start aside like a deceitful bow. A besieged city, when the besiegers have friends within the walls, that are ready to lay hold of any opportunity to betray it, the inhabitants had need to be more circumspect and vigilant. Such a city is the emblem of a believer; though his heart is renewed, yet it is only in part, it remains still in part corrupted, and that corruption sides with the tempter, and is ready to yield and open to him. Therefore, faithfulness to the Lord and to himself is often to be pressed on the Christian.

2. Shaking temptations are likely to be met with. "The rain will descend, and the floods come, and the winds blow and beat on the house," (Matthew 7:27) to try whether it is founded on a rock, or on the sand only.

1. This charge to be faithful is very requisite, if we consider that in time of shaking, many will take offense, and depart from Christ. Christians in show will then discover their want of faith and love in truth. And when these fall off, the saints had need to be cautioned. "Do not you also leave me." So that they may reply with Peter, "Lord, to whom shall we go? Thou hast the words of eternal life," (John 6:67-68); and eternal life itself to bestow on us.

In the further handling of this doctrine, I shall first show what it is to be faithful. Secondly, I shall give good and sufficient reason why a Christian should be faithful.

In the first place, I am to show what it is to be faithful. This apostle briefly and yet excellently sets forth, "This charge I commit unto thee son Timothy, according to the prophesies which went before on thee, that by them thou mightest war a good warfare, holding faith and a good conscience," (1 Timothy 1:18). And in holding these, we hold all that is worth our care to secure.

The epithet "precious" is given to faith, "To them who have obtained the precious faith with us," (2 Peter 1:1). And if you would know how precious, you have it, (1 Peter 1:7). Faith is not only said to be as precious as gold, but much more precious than gold, even much more precious than gold that perishes, therefore it is to be held fast.

FIVE THINGS IMPLIED

Now in holding the faith, these five things are implied. We hold fast. First, the doctrine. Second, the object. Third, the confidence. Fourth, the life. Fifth, the profession of our faith without wavering.

1. He that is faithful holds fast the doctrine of faith. He looks on the truths of Christ as worth buying at any rate. Buy the truth, and do not sell it, said wise Solomon. Truth is of God; a bright and glorious beam, that shines from the sun of righteousness. Truth is a Christian's pilot, his compass; he will quickly split on some rock, or sink in some sand; if this is not heeded, the Christian is in a dark place, where stumbling blocks and snares are innumerably many. And the truth of Christ, the doctrine of faith is a light to his feet, and a lamp to his paths. The church of Pergamos, though Satan hurts them, Christ says, you hold fast my name, "and hast not decayed my faith," (Revelation 2:13); that is, my doctrine, which I delivered to be believed and obeyed. Rather than the Gospel should be let go, and buried in silence, we must venture all for its propagation. Even peace itself we are to endeavor after no further than consists with truth. The apostle did not care what troubles and stir the Gospel caused, and though Satan and the ungodly stormed at the light, they boldly published that message which they had a command to deliver. *As long as*

the Gospel lives and thrives; no matter what disturbances are created by its enemies.

2. He that is faithful holds fast the object of faith. Now the object of faith is laid down, "Ye believe in God, believe also in me," (John 14:1) says Christ to his disciples. It is our duty and our safety to cleave to the only true God, and Jesus Christ whom he has sent. A believer keeps his hold of God, who is his shield, and exceeding great reward; who can defend him from evil, or turn those evils which he feels to his advantage, who can crown him with lovingkindness, and such mercies as are tender, suitable, satisfactory and sure. Neither will he let go of his hold of Jesus Christ, who has brought him near, and keeps him near to this God, who guides him by his Spirit, who by virtue of his blood and intercession, is continually making up the breaches that the believer's sinful infirmities make; and who out of his fullness is ready to impart whatever grace in any time of need is necessary.

3. He that is faithful holds fast his assurance and confidence of faith. After he has given all diligence to attain assurance, he is loathe to lose what cost him such pains to get. The apostle presses this again and again, "But Christ as a Son over his own house, whose house we are," if we hold fast the confidence and "rejoicing of hope firm unto the end," (Hebrews 3:6). "Cast not away therefore your confidence which hath great recompense of reward." Assurance of faith is

a mighty support in the evil day. The eye of faith when faith is heightened to a full persuasion and confidence, will look through the clouds and behold God smiling when men frown. Faith will hear God speaking peace in a still voice, when the mouths of men are full of threatenings and furious rebukes. Faith will perceive the better substance enduring, when earthly goods are taken away.

But when troubles on earth surround us on every side, and we are at uncertainties, of what our lot will be in the next world. When there are fightings without, and in reference to our spiritual estate, doubts and fears within, this will render our condition doleful. O therefore labor and pray for assurance, do not cherish any distemper of heart, give no place to the devil, for this doing will feed your fears, and strengthen your unbelief.

4. He that is faithful holds fast the life of faith. As this is the safest, so it is the sweetest life on earth. Those that walk by sight and not by faith, will presently grow faith and weary in the hour of temptation. If flesh and blood are consulted with, if our murmuring and repining senses are heeded, we shall refuse to row against the stream, and be carried away with the corruption of the times we live in. If Moses had been led by sense, his choice and practice would have been contrary to what it was. Sense would have prized honor, and so he would have still been called the son of Pharaoh's daughter.

Sense would have coveted wealth and delight, so he would have had his heart glued to the pleasure of sin, and the treasures of Egypt. But Moses walked by faith, and therefore chose to suffer afflictions with the people of God, he esteemed it part of his riches to be reproached for Christ, for faith continually showed "Him that is invisible," and "the recompense of reward to him," (Hebrews 11:24-27).

So the apostle walked by faith, and professes, "I am crucified with Christ, nevertheless I live, yet not I, but Christ liveth in me; and the life which I now live in the flesh, I live by the faith of the Son of God, who loved me, and gave himself for me," (Galatians 2:20). Those that live by faith stay themselves on the promises of sustentation, and no weight can sink them. They cast their burdens and themselves on the Lord, who being faithful, will not suffer them to be tempted above what they are able.

5. He that is faithful holds fast the profession of his faith. He heeds that admonition of the apostle, "Let us hold fast the profession of our faith without wavering, for he is faithful that hath promised," (Hebrews 10:25). He is not ashamed of his Lord and Master, he even esteems it an honor for his Master's sake to be despised. Though the kings and rulers of the earth take counsel, and set themselves against the Lord's Christ, yet the faithful servant will stick to him. He is not ashamed to be of that way that is everywhere spoken against; he is not

ashamed of that Gospel, which is a stumbling block to the Jews, to the Greeks foolishness; he is not ashamed of that word which "a sinful and adulterous generation reproach, and have no delight in it," (Jeremiah 6:10).

His principal care and study indeed is to be a sincere lover, and real practicer of religion; and yet he is not afraid to be an open professor, though thereby it comes to pass that he is evilly entreated by enemies of religion. That is the first thing implied in being faithful, namely *holding faith*.

2. To be faithful is also to hold a good conscience. When Paul stood before the council, earnestly beholding them, he protested, "I have lived in all good conscience before God unto this day," (Acts 23:1). Also see Acts 24:16. Herein I exercise myself to have a conscience void of offense towards God and towards men. The unsteadiest professor does not regard his conscience, and makes nothing of wounding and defiling it. But the faithful soul speaks much of what the same language with holy Job, "Till I die I will not remove my integrity from me; my righteousness I hold fast, and will not let it go, my heart shall not reproach me so long as I live," (Job 27:5-6).

THREE THINGS THAT ARGUE A GOOD CONSCIENCE

There are these three things that argue a good conscience:

1. Where the conscience is good, no sinful designs are carried on. Sinister aims are not allowed by one that is faithful. If his treacherous heart begins to have a squinted eye at his own praise or profit, he checks it presently. What he does, he designs that God may have the glory of; and surely the glory is the Lord's due, since his strengthening grace does all in us, and for us. And by suffering, the faithful man does not aim at the advancing of his own repute, but that Christ may be magnified by his trials, his patience and joy in them. And if the world is convinced, the weak confirmed, if the Gospel gets ground, and the Lord Jesus is prized and admired by a greater multitude, he has his end and purpose.

2. Where the conscience is good, ungodly desires are not harbored. He that is faithful looks well to his desires, that they be preserved pure. The world is undesirable, sin is abominable, but his "soul thirsteth for God for the living God," (Psalm 42:2) and sufferings are willingly undergone, so this thirst may be satisfied.

3. Where conscience is good, it is purged from dead works. "How much more shall the blood of Christ, who through the eternal Spirit offered himself without spot to

God, purge your consciences from dead works to serve the living God?" (Hebrews 9:14). A good conscience will not wink at unwarrantable practices, will not connive at not doing the work of the Lord or doing that work negligently. He that is faithful makes conscience to walk before God in truth, though never so many in their works deny the Lord. He is grieved and vexed at other's filthy conversation, and orders his own aright; and so though for a while he is used hardly, "he comes at length to see the salvation of God," (Psalm 50:23).

WHY A CHRISTIAN SHOULD BE FAITHFUL

In the second place, I am to lay down the reasons why a Christian should be faithful.

1. A Christian is under a command to be faithful. And this command to be steadfast, is very much expressed and pressed in Scripture. "Be steadfast, unmoveable, always abounding in the work of the Lord," (1 Corinthians 15:58). "So stand fast in the Lord my dearly beloved," (Philippians 4:1). "Watch ye stand fast in the faith, quit ye like men," (1 Corinthians 16:13). "Jesus said unto them that believed on him; if ye continue in my word, then are ye my disciples indeed," (John 8:31). Moses likewise of old, harped on this string; commanding the children of Israel not only to turn, but to cleave to the Lord, "That thou mayest love the Lord thy God,

and obey his voice, and cleave unto him, for he is thy life," (Deuteronomy 30:20). And they are forbidden to turn either to the right hand or to the left from following the Lord their God. Now all these commandments the Christian's obligation to faithfulness the stronger; and truly to be unfaithful is not a single sin, for he that leaves the Lord, how fearfully must he be drawn into transgression.

2. A Christian is under *covenant* to be faithful, (Deuteronomy 26:17). He had avouched the Lord to be his God. He was given up to God before, and how often has he made of himself a fresh resignation, on days of humiliation? And when he has eaten and drank at the Lord's table, his covenant to be the Lord's has been renewed. How often has the Christian professed that his heart and members were not his own, but God's, to dwell in and to make use of. This is another reason, why he should be faithful. The Lord is the Christian's, and the Christian is the Lord's portion. "The Lord's portion is his people, and Jacob is the lot of his inheritance." Now God's inheritance should be for his use, and should in no wise be alienated.

3. The God of believers is faithful, therefore they should resemble him. The Scripture speaks in a glorious strain concerning the faithfulness of God. He is said to keep truth forever. The hills and mountains do not stand as firm as his covenant shall. "For the mountains shall depart, and the hills

be removed, but my kindness shall not depart from thee, nor the covenant of my peace be removed, saith the Lord that hath mercy on thee," (Leviticus 54:10). No, the Scripture goes much higher than the mountains in setting forth this faithfulness, "I have said, mercy shall be built up forever; Thy faithfulness shalt thou establish in the very heavens." And being thus established, nothing on earth can shake this faithfulness, it will be as apparent and illustrious as the heavens are. The ordinances of heaven, as the sun by day, and of the moon and stars by night, are not more unalterable than the Lord's covenant, (Jeremiah 31:33-36).

4. The Lord is glorified by a Christian's proving faithful. It reflects dishonor on him when his servants leave him. O then how faithful should they be? The world's prejudices against the Lord's service are heightened, and they are hardened in their stubborn and evil way, when they behold professors apostatizing, and become their companions again in the paths of folly and wickedness. But the faithful man causes the way of truth to be well spoken of, by his faithfulness he proclaims his Master's goodness and his power, and in both ways is his Master glorified.

1. He proclaims his Master's goodness, and that he has made the best choice, since he will suffer anything rather than part with his Lord. The Israelitish servant that refused to go out free at the year of release, and had his ear bored through

with an awl, was a plain demonstration of his Master's kindness, since liberty was not so much esteemed at his service. And so when we are unmovable in our Lord's work, we proclaim the world that our Master is exceedingly gracious; and who knows but that by this means the number of his servants may be increased?

2. The man that is faithful proclaims his Lord's power. The power of Christ rests on him, else he would be unstable as water, who through Christ's strengthening of him is like the very Rock unshaken; and the more weak the believer is, the more glorious is his power in whom he believes.

APPLICATION OF THE SEVENTH DOCTRINE

Use 1. Of reproofs, and I shall direct it to two sorts of persons.

1. The fickle and inconstant are to be reproved. Their spirit is unsteadfast with the Lord, if the world makes proffer of its good things, or threatens them with evil. Vain hopes draw them away, vain fears drive them away from Christ. Sometimes they seem to be his humble servants; but this is only a hypocritical kind of compliment; they are resolved to serve, please, and to secure, *whatever* becomes of Christ, his honor and his Gospel.

2. They are to be reproved that are in an ill sense unfaithful; faithful to their sins, which are the worst masters; unlovable in their resolution to make provision for the flesh, to fulfill the lusts of it. There is a strange stoutness of spirit, and fixedness in evil, that is to be found in thousands. "Their neck is like an iron sinew, their brow like brass; they make their faces harder than a rock, they refuse to return." Say what we will, sin is their master, and sin they will serve, though they be told a hundred and a hundred times that death is its wages. They are as unchangeable in evil as the spots of the leopard, or the blackness of the Ethiopian. O that we would learn of sin's vassals, to be as faithful to the best, as they are to the worst lord.

Use 2. Of exhortation. Let me press you to be faithful.

1. How many obligations lie on you to be steadfast? Infinite millions of encouragements are given to you. The more constant, the more comfort and peace is found. "Great peace have they," says David, "that love thy law, and nothing shall offend them." Every mercy of those many thousands you receive, should be a cord to tie you faster to God; and what strange kind of hearts you have, if so many cords are snapped asunder, and so many obligations are forgotten.

2. Whom do you leave when you are unfaithful? You forsake that Lord, whose lovingkindness is so excellent, who is able to perform all things for you, whose all sufficiency can

furnish you though never so indigent. This God you leave, and for what do you leave him? Is it for that which is not bread? It is for that "which can never satisfy," (Isaiah 55:2).

3. By faithfulness you not only deprive yourselves of the Lord's goodness, but engage him against you. "His hands are on all them for good that seek him, but his power and his wrath is against those that forsake him," (Ezra 8:22). And wrath armed with such power is dreadful. God greatly abhors the backslider. When his ancient people "turned back and dealt unfaithfully like their fathers," it is said, "When the Lord heard this he was wroth, and greatly abhorred Israel," (Psalm 78:57,59).

4. If you are faithful with God, you shall find by experience his ways to be truth and mercy. "All the paths of the Lord are mercy and truth, unto such as keep his covenant and his testimonies," (Psalm 25:10). His promises you shall experience to be true; his mercies will all in mercy be bestowed; no there will be mercy in every affliction, in every distress, mercy supporting, mercy reviving, mercy turning all things to the best. As the philosophers stone is said to turn all metals into gold.

Use 3. Of direction how to be made faithful.

1. Be sensible of the treachery of your own spirits, and let this make you the more jealous of yourselves all your days. "Watch ye, stand fast," says the apostle. If you would stand

fast, you must be exceedingly vigilant. Watch that nothing may come in at the door of your senses, which may prove a snare; and that nothing go out of your heart which may defile you. When first the heart begins to grow weary of well-doing, or to hearken to the tempter, observe it, and being apprehensive of your danger, cry to be quickened and established.

2. Pray to be upheld by the Spirit of the Lord. So did David, (Psalm 51:12). Restore to me the joy of your salvation, and uphold me with your free Spirit. Where the Spirit of the Lord is, there is liberty, life, holiness, strength. Do not grieve the Spirit, but be obsequious to him, and he will strengthen you with might in your inward man. When Christ was about to go away, and part with his disciples, he promised to send the Spirit, who should abide with them forever; and it was by this Spirit that they were born up and carried through all their work, and the difficulties that attended it.

3. Plead the covenant, one clause of this is, "I will not turn away from them to do them good, and I will put my fear into their hearts that they shall not depart from me," (Jeremiah 32:40). Again he says, "Thou shalt call me my Father, and shalt not depart from me," (Jeremiah 3:19). Prize these promises, plead them, believe them, and as sure as God is faithful, he will make you faithful whatever your sufferings

or temptations are.

THE EIGHTH DOCTRINE

The eighth doctrine is that a Christian's faithfulness must run parallel with his life, to the death he must be "steadfast."

The Greek word for *steadfast* may have a double interpretation.

1. Be faithful to the death, that is, be unlovable, though it costs you your life to be so. Do not prefer your life before that Lord who laid down his life to redeem you from death, and who will recompense the loss of life temporal with that life that is everlasting. A Christian is to resist, even to blood, striving against sin, as the apostle speaks; he must choose rather to part with his blood, than to lose his God.

2. Be faithful to the death, that is, be faithful all your days; that when death comes, and the Lord by death, he may find you doing his work, doubling his talents, standing up for his interest, notwithstanding all derision and opposition.

The reasons why we should be faithful to the death are *these:*

1. Much of the former part of our life has been lost; therefore all the remainder should be the more faithfully

devoted to God. The time past of our life may more than suffice to have dishonored him; therefore all the "rest of our time in the flesh, should be lived, not to the lusts of men (either our own lusts, or the lusts of others) but to the will of God," (1 Peter 4:2-3). The whole was his due, let him not be denied that part which is behind.

2. The longer we know our Lord, and the closer we keep to him, the better we shall like him; therefore it is but reason that to the last we should be steadfast. Cardinal Wolsey indeed was weary of the service of King Henry VIII, and said, "If he had served God so faithfully as he had done the king, God would not have forsaken him in his gray hairs." But Christ is another kind of Master than any other potentate. Old Polycarp said that he had "served Christ for several scores of years, and knew nothing but good by him," and therefore in his old age he chose to suffer anything rather than deny him. The harder we follow after Christ, and the longer we continue as his disciples, we discover new beauties, new pleasures, new treasures, and so we can never find just reason to exchange, since it will be so much for the worse; but just reason to the contrary, since Christ's loveliness, fullness, and liberality in communicating of that fullness, daily more and more abundantly appears.

3. If we are not faithful to the death, all that we have done before will be lost; we shall lose those things which we

have wrought, and miss our reward. Here is a full place, "But when the righteous man turneth away from his righteousness, and commiteth iniquity, and doth according to all the abominations that the wicked man doth, shall he live? All his righteousness that he hath done shall not be mentioned; in his trespass that he hath trespassed, and in his sin which he hath sinned, in them shall he die," (Ezekiel 18:24). By the righteous man we are to understand one that by his profession is righteous, and outwardly blameless, performing the duties required of him; if he gives out and turns aside, all his duties will be lost, all his hearing, all his prayers, all his deeds of justice and mercy will not be mentioned; he does not continue steadfast, which shows that he was never sincere, however others were deceived by him, and himself too.

APPLICATION OF THE EIGHTH DOCTRINE

Use 1. The only use of this doctrine shall be to admonish all that profess the name of Christ, to persevere to the end. Depart from iniquity, but never from your Lord. When first you give up yourselves to Christ, reckon on this, that you must ever abide with him. Your closing with Christ is a marriage, and this husband never dies, you must not give away yourselves to another. The arguments to persuade you to be faithful till death are these:

1. Many unfaithful ones at death tremble and are in horror because of their apostasy. Conscience often awakens when the king of terrors is within view. A dreadful sound is in the backslider's ears, trouble and anguish make him afraid and prevail against him, as a king ready for battle. To have one's spirit wounded with an intolerable stroke, to have the devil's accusing, the creature's all failing, has set in order before the eyes, calamity *as a storm* ready to hurl one out of the world, and God so far from pitying as to laugh at one's destruction, and to "be comforted in the vengeance that is inflicted," (Ezekiel 5:13) must necessarily be very dreadful. But this is the doleful case and conclusion of many backsliders.

2. Death is near at hand, do not think much of so short a time to be faithful. If a Master should say, "Work hard today, and I will give you an inheritance for your life," truly the most slothful would not think much of the heat and burden. Now God says, "abide in my service for a little while, and then you shall rest from all your labors and sufferings, and that rest shall be forever." O how should this encourage!

3. Faithfulness to the death will take away the fear of death. Death will be looked on as a messenger to tell you that your Lord can no longer brook your absence, to tell you that your warfare is accomplished; and that having been faithful in your Master's business, you must enter into your Master's joy. Be faithful to death, and Christ will stand by you at death, and

after death he will receive you.

THE NINTH DOCTRINE

The ninth doctrine is that on those that continue faithful to death, Christ will certainly bestow a crown of life and immortality.

If the eye of faith was more open and strong sighted, how would this crown glisten and shine? What a vehement inducement would it prove to perseverance?

In the handling of this doctrine, I shall first endeavor to show what matter of life the text speaks of. Secondly, in what regard this life is called a crown. Thirdly, lay down some arguments to prove the certainty of the doctrine, that the faithful shall be thus crowned with immortality, then close with the uses.

In the first place I am to show what manner of life the text speaks of. A subject I confess, more fit for an angel's tongue than mine. The soul while imprisoned in the body is of a narrow capacity; and apprehends only a little of that glory which is above. The actual inhabitants of the New Jerusalem can best tell what kind of habitation it is. Those that are only passing through the wilderness of this world, know only a little of what manner of life is led in the heavenly Canaan; yet since we have a map of this blessed land of promise, in the

Word, let us take a view of it, and let us view so long, until we cry with Augustine's mother, *Quid hic facimus? What do we here?* And groan with pangs of desire to be gone from here and possessed of our heavenly country. Now, what the word speaks of this life above, I shall declare in these *particulars*:

1. That life above will consist in the nearest union and conjunction to God. Natural life is the result of union between the soul and body, and eternal life, of the union between the soul and God. And truly to be banished and separated from the Lord forever, will be the second death. The apostle comforts the Thessalonians with this, "So shall we ever be with the Lord," (Thessalonians 2:17). How near their God will the saints be admitted hereafter? His dwelling in them is comparatively called an absence, in respect of that presence in the other world to be vouchsafed. These three things will be consequent on this union to *God*:

1. One will be the vision or seeing of God, says the apostle. "For now we see through a glass darkly, but then face to face; now I know in part, but then I shall know even as also I am known," (1 Corinthians 13:12). The saints shall no longer complain of darkness, of ignorance, of those *horribiles dubitationes* as *Melancthon* calls them, horrible doublings concerning God, with which they are sometimes haunted. They shall see God immediately, and what they behold, how

will it raise their love, joy, and wonder! The Lord said to Moses, "Thou canst not see my face and live." Such a sight would be so glorious as that your frail nature would be overwhelmed by it. But the perfected saints are strengthened for such a felicity, their life lies in loping and gazing at him; whose glory should it only shine forth, would overwhelm the most sanctified mortal here on earth."

And when the face of God is seen, the soul is all light, all love. All the excellencies and beauties in the creatures by which affection is attracted, in comparison of what is to be seen in God, are not so much as the thousandth part of the least spark of fire, compared with the sun when it shines in its greatest strength and noontide glory. The face of God will then be smoothe, not one frown to be seen, not one look that will manifest the least displeasure. Nothing but smiles and glorious aspects, which will evidently show the incomprehensible greatness of his love and joy that he takes in, who are the perfectly purified vessels of glory.

2. Another consequent of this union to God will be likeness to him. "But as for me," says David, "I will behold thy face in righteousness; I shall be satisfied when I awake with thy likeness," (Psalm 17:15). The sight of God will be transforming, and that likeness will cause abundant satisfaction. The beholding of the Lord in his ordinances, does in a degree, "change us into the same image from glory to

glory," (2 Corinthians 3:18) and this much more the beholding of him in his kingdom. "Beloved, now are we the sons of God, and it doth not yet appear what we shall be, but we know, that when he shall appear, we shall be like him, for we shall see him as he is," (1 John 3:2). Then the Image of God begun here will be completed. Here, it is only like a rude draught, like a picture in dead colors; but then the piece will have had God's last hand on it, the work will be finished; and O how exactly alike will all the children be to their holy and heavenly Father? Now they hunger and thirst after righteousness; but then the promise of filling them will be fulfilled and performed to the uttermost.

3. Another consequent of this union to God will be the enjoyment of him. The saints pant after the Lord now, as the chased hart after the water brooks; but in glory they shall have as much of God as they can desire, or contain, the Holy Spirit tells us that God will be "all in all," (1 Corinthians 15:28). All that they can wish, all sufficient to fill them to the brim. The goodness, and power, and faithfulness, and love of God, have sometimes deep and sweet impressions on the saints now. But what will the impressions be then? How durable, how transporting? They shall lie, as it were, with their heads at the fountain of living waters perpetually; no thirst, no scantiness will be complained of. These are the consequents of that near union and communion to God,

wherein this life above will consist.

2. That life above will be most holy and unspotted. Sin will be pardoned, cleansed and abolished. *Filia devorabit Matrem,* Death the daughter will put an end to sin the mother. Believers, though alive by grace, carry a body of death about with them, which makes the condition somewhat like theirs who fell into the hands of the tyrant of old called *Mizentins,* who joined the members of a living man to a dead carcass, the hands, and breast, and face of the one, to those of the other (*Mortua jungebat corpora vivis Componens manibusque manus, atq, oribus ora. Virg.*). But when the saints have come to glory, the body of death will be killed though the natural body will be raised, yet the body of sin will never have a resurrection. Instead of, "O wretched! Who shall deliver us?" will be, "glory and everlasting praise to him who hath made us free from sin, the worst of evils, and from all the lesser miseries that attend it!" The spouse of Christ will then be "presented a glorious church, not having spot, or wrinkle, or any such thing. But it will be holy and without blemish," (Ephesians 5:27). Then the blood of Christ will have had its perfect operation. The saints will be washed white as snow, they will look as white, or whiter than Adam did in innocence. All spots will be done off. Every wrinkle will be smoothed, and the members, every one of them, will be like their Head; altogether lovely. The church

is now as fair as the moon, it has spots with its fairness, sometimes it waxes, sometimes it wanes; but when it is translated to heaven, it will be clear as the sun itself, (Song of Solomon 6:10).

3. That life above will be most sweet and pleasant. The saints shall no longer cry out vanity and vexation of spirit; as they did when under the sun. "But God will wipe away all tears from their eyes, and there shall be no more death, neither sorrow nor crying, neither shall there be anymore pain, for the former things being passed away," (Revelation 21:4). When they come to live in the presence of God, their joy will be so full, as to be incapable of any addition, when they are at God's right hand, their pleasures will be forever. Even in this veil of tears there is a peace attained which passes all understanding, a joy that is unspeakable and full of glory. So that the saints mouths are full of songs in the house of their pilgrimage. O then how short and unsuitable are our apprehensions of the pleasures dealt forth in the heavenly paradise!

4. That life above will be most secure and safe. Dangers will then be all gone through. When we are entering into the gate of the New Jerusalem, we shall shake hands with all the enemies that before molested us, and not so much as one of them will be able to follow us. The great gulf between us and them, will keep them off at an everlasting distance. There will be no danger, either from within or from without. No serpent

in that paradise to tempt man again to fall from his restored innocence. The heart will confer in goodness, it will never have the least inclination to decline from God. There will be no need of that vigilance and standing on our guard, that now is necessary; for our hearts will be perfectly cured of their deceitfulness, and there will be no adversaries to lay snares for us.

5. That life above will be most quiet and peaceable. It is not improbable that in the latter days there will be a more peaceable church state, than as yet there has been; when that promise and others of the like nature will be more visibly accomplished. "But with righteousness shall he judge the poor, and reprove with equity for the meek of the earth: and he shall smite the earth with the rod of his mouth, and with the breath of his lips shall he slay the wicked. And righteousness shall be the girdle of his loins, and faithfulness the girdle of his reins. The wolf also shall dwell with the lamb, and the leopard shall lie down with the kid; and the calf and the young lion and the fatling together; and a little child shall lead them. And the cow and the bear shall feed; their young ones shall lie down together: and the lion shall eat straw like the ox. And the sucking child shall play on the hole of the asp, and the weaned child shall put his hand on the cockatrice' den. They shall not hurt nor destroy in all my holy mountain: for the earth shall be full of the knowledge of the LORD, as

the waters cover the sea," (Isaiah 11:4-9). But most certainly this peace and concord shall be among the saints above; no biting, no devouring one another, no diversity of judgments, but all will agree in the same truth; no alienation of affection, for love to the Lord, and to one another will be perfect; the spirit that lusts to envy will be cast out, selfish ends will carry none aside, disputes will be at an end, the wounds which divisions have made will be closed. How good and pleasant will be that unity, when all the saints will be of one and of the right mind.

6. That life above will be led among the most suitable society. The saints will then have bid farewell to Meschech and the tents of Kedar; they shall no longer dwell among revilers at holiness, the openly profane, the scandalous or lifeless professors of religion; no filthy communication or conversation in heaven to vex their righteous souls; no contempt of God, no provoking the eyes of his glory; no cursing, swearing, pride, wantonness, to be heard or seen in the heavenly city. When they come there, they will say, "How blessedly unlike is this, to that place and company which we came from." Glorified spirits, innumerable companies of angels will be their companions, these will be glad to see them safely arrived to rest. For if there is joy in heaven at the conversion of a sinner, we may very well infer that there will be joy likewise at the saints coronation.

7. That life above will fully answer its end. The saints were formed by the Lord for himself, and they will be eternally showing forth his praise and glory. They will never entertain so much as an unbecoming thought of God; but to magnify and extol him will be their everlasting business; their hearts and their harps will be ever in tune to sound forth his Name. Now they lisp and stammer out his praises; but then how seraphical will their songs be? And they will never be weary of singing hallelujahs. O what ecstasies of joy and love; with what ravishment of spirit, with what inconceivable raptures of delight will the whole assembly and church of the firstborn join together, saying, "Amen, blessing, and glory, and wisdom, and thanksgiving, and honor, and power, and might be to our God forever and ever, Amen," (Revelation 7:12). The triumphant saints will perfectly answer the design of God, in their creation, in their new creation; they will glorify him forever, who on them has bestowed eternal glory.

8. The life above will be an *everlasting* life. Death itself will be destroyed and swallowed up in victory. The eternity of the saint's joys and enjoyments makes them infinitely of greater value. Heaven would no longer be heaven, if they ever were to be turned out of it; all the sweetness would be embittered with the thoughts of its period. But may the riches of mercy be adored, for the inheritance is said to be incorruptible, the kingdom cannot be moved, the crown of

glory does not fade away; "the gift of God is eternal life, through Christ Jesus our Lord," (Romans 6:23).

Now you damned spirits, your miseries are everlasting, you are banished from God, and shall never be called back; but will be unconsumed fuel for unquenchable flames. Triumph and rejoice you glorious souls. As long as God is, he will be your God, your portion, your reward; as long as God is, you shall live in his presence and enjoy him. Thus you see what manner of life the text speaks of.

How This Life is Called a Crown

In the second place I am to show on what score this life is called a crown.

1. This crown intimates that the saints are conquerors. They have run the race, and won the prize; they have fought the good fight of faith, and laid hold on eternal life. They may truly say *Super-superamus*, we are more than conquerors. They have, being strengthened by he that loves them, conquered the whole world, conquered the principalities and powers of hell, conquered themselves too, their own lusts and passions, and affections. All other battles are petty skirmishes to the spiritual combat; mortal men are but inconsiderable enemies compared with fleshly lusts and evil angels. All the

conquerors recorded in history are hardly worth the mentioning with a Christian that endures and overcomes. And what is *laurel* to that crown at last put on the Christian's head?

2. This crown speaks the honor and dignity whereunto the saints are advanced. Though exceedingly filled with contempt and the scorning of those that are at ease, yet even here the saints are kings and priests. "Unto him that loved us, and washed us from our sins in his own blood, and hath made us kings and priests unto God and his Father; to him be glory and dominion forever and ever," (Revelation 1:5-6). And when they come to glory, they are actually crowned; it is evident that the world was not worthy of them, and that far better than what the world could bestow, is freely given to them. Heaven is called a kingdom, the reward a crown, to show it is no mean price that the Christian aims at. What is all the height and grandeur on earth to the kingly dignity put on believers? What are all the kingdoms of the world, and the glory of them, compared to reigning with the Lord forever? The four great monarchies by the Holy Spirit are compared to the four great beasts, (Daniel 7:3). Surely earthly crowns are only base and sordid to the heavenly.

3. This expression, a crown if life, is used to show that the crown does not fade, will never be less bright for wearing, will never be thrown off, it is a living crown, a crown of

immortality.

THE SAINTS SHALL BE CROWNED

In the next place follows the arguments to prove the doctrine that the saints shall be thus crowned; and they are *these*:

1. One shall be drawn from the Father's good pleasure. This good pleasure Christ declares to the little flocks' encouragement. "Fear not little flock, it is your Father's good pleasure to give you the kingdom," (Luke 12:32). And his counsel is immutable, he will do his pleasure. This pleasure he has plainly signified in his covenant and promises, wherein glory as well as grace is assured; and hereby he has heightened believers' hopes and expectations; and certainly to frustrate them is not consistent with his truth and goodness.

2. A second argument shall be drawn from Christ's purchase; He has purchased that possession for his saints in the next world; he has bought that crown by his cross. In the new testament, the Lord Jesus has bequeathed life to them, and "by the death of himself, the testator, thus testament is confirmed," (Hebrews 9:16). So that this life is as sure, as it is sure that our Lord died.

3. A third argument shall be drawn from Christ's

entering into life, and taking possession of the kingdom. He lives, and was dead, and behold, he is alive forevermore. He is set down with his Father in his throne, and has gone there partly to this end, that he might fit crowns and prepare mansions for his persevering followers, (Job 14:2).

4. A fourth argument shall be drawn from the foretaste of this glorious life that at present are vouchsafed. Spiritual life is eternal life in the bud, and the bud will at length be fully blown. In ordinances a heaven on earth is sometimes enjoyed. O then how are the things unseen made evident! When faith and spiritual sense and experience go together, then there is that which the apostle calls a "full assurance of understanding," (Colossians 2:2).

5. A fifth argument shall be drawn from the earnest of the Spirit. "In whom after that ye believed, ye were sealed with that Holy Spirit of promise, which is the earnest of our inheritance until the redemption of the purchased possession to the praise of his glory," (Ephesians 1:13-14). And in other places we read of the earnest of the Spirit. The Spirit of wisdom and revelation makes the saints know what is the hope of their calling, and what the riches of their glorious inheritance are. And the Lord gives his Spirit, not only to reveal this to them, but as an earnest and pledge to assure them of it, and that after they are made fit to be partakers of

the life and glory which he has promised, they shall undoubtedly enjoy it.

APPLICATION OF THE NINTH DOCTRINE

At last I come to the *uses*:

Use 1. Of instruction. We may learn the woeful condition of the ungodly. There is a crown, but not for them. A glorious life above, but they shall die the everlasting death. By the ungodly, I mean those that allow themselves in sin, which the Word and conscience tells them they ought to cast away. Not only the open unbeliever, but the secret hypocrite is concerned, who is an unbeliever as well as the other. When these read of heaven's joys, it should fill them with sorrow to consider that their "triumph will be but short, and their joy will last but for a moment," (Job 20:5). There are these five things that will exceedingly aggravate the loss of life to the ungodly.

1. This life was proffered often to the ungodly in the Gospel. The fountain of living waters was not a sealed fountain, but it was open; and yet this fountain was forsaken for the sake of broken cisterns. The Spirit and the bride say come, and the sinners pressing necessity and lack say *go*, and drink of the waters of life, since you may do it freely,

(Revelation 22:17) and yet he *refuses* to accept the invitation. Pardon goes, as it were, a begging, and glory a begging in the Gospel, and yet neither are accepted, though offered on terms most just and reasonable. O how will it torture the damned to reflect on this, that they would not come to Christ, though life was assured on their coming, (Job 5:40).

2. It will heighten the misery of undone sinners to consider what they preferred before this crown of life. O where were their wits when sin was cherished in their hearts, while Christ stood at the door? When the world that is so empty, so unstable, so ensnaring, was looked on as a better inheritance than that which is incorruptible.

3. Some that perish have been not far from the kingdom. The Spirit of God has strived; their own spirits have been startled, and almost persuaded to turn indeed; and if they had done so, they would have lived, this crown would have been their own. But some sin or another was a cord to hold them fast; some command wherein suffering, self-denial, strictness is enjoined, made them first demur, then consulting with flesh and blood, to take offense at Christ, and so away. And it is a heightening of misery to have been near to happiness and through our own fault and folly to have missed it.

4. The ungodly hereafter will have other apprehensions of this crown which they have slighted. When they see the prophets, apostles, and saints in the kingdom, and perceive

what a luster their crowns have; what bliss and glory is their portion; O how will they grow mad at themselves for grief and vexation, that they were so sottishly ignorant, to condemn such a treasure.

5. Despair of ever gaining that crown of life will seize on them. Now there is hope, but hereafter the door of heaven, and the door of hope will too be shut, and never be opened again. No prayers will be heard, no tears will move compassion. Christ, the giver of life, will say, "depart ye cursed;" and the invitation to come to him will be heard no more forever. How will desperation torture them, when they consider that they have lost, and how their loss is irreparable. They lived as fools, and they died as fools, and then after, wisdom cannot at all avail them.

Bring these things to mind, consider and show yourselves men, O you transgressors. When life and death were set before you, why should death as the best of the two be chosen?

Use 2. Of examination. It highly concerns all to examine whether they have a right to this crown of life, or not. Most expect it, but most will be ashamed of their ungrounded hope and expectation. To help you against deceiving your own souls in this self-examination, I shall describe those that have a title to this crown, that are indeed the heirs of life, by these ensuing characters:

1. Those who have a right to the crown of life are believers on the Son of God. "He that believeth on the Son of God hath everlasting life." What is it to believe on Christ? It is to receive him as he is offered in the Gospel. How is Christ offered in the Gospel? As a Prince, and as a Savior. Christ cannot be received as a Prince, but the dominion of sin must be pulled down. He cannot be received as a Savior, but our own righteousness and strength must be looked on as insufficient and invaluable to salvation. He that thus has accepted the Son, has life by him. "This is the record that God has given us eternal life, and this life is in his Son," (1 John 5:11) seek it elsewhere and you will never find it.

2. Those who are heirs to the crown of life, are quickened by the Spirit. It is the Spirit that quickens, (John 6:63). Sometime they were dead in trespasses and sins; but God who is rich in mercy, for the great love with which he loved them, quickened them by the Holy Spirit, (Ephesians 2:4). They are alive to God. His Spirit dwells in them, they breathe after him, they walk in his ways; they do his work, they aim at his glory. And this spiritual life is the forerunner of, and preparative to that which is eternal.

3. Those who are heirs to the crown of life diligently hearken to the word of God, they are willing to be reproved for sin, to be instructed concerning duty; they hear, they keep the word as well as hear it. "He is in the way of life that

keepeth instruction," (Proverbs 10:17). So, "For the commandment is a lamp, and the law is a light, and the reproofs of instruction is the way of life," (Proverbs 6:23). The word of God has only a convincing and covering, and an edifying power, but it will put the crown at last on the head of the faithful. Therefore, the apostle affirms it, "able to give the inheritance." "And now brethren I commend you to God, and to the word of his grace, which is able to build you up, and to give you an inheritance among all them that are sanctified," (Acts 20:32).

4. Those who are heirs to the crow of life, mortify the deeds of the body; by the Spirit's help they do it. "If ye live after the flesh, ye shall die; but if ye through the Spirit do mortify the deeds of the body, ye shall live. The heirs of life are weary of the body of sin and death; therefore they crucify the flesh with the affections and lusts of it. They mortify their members on earth, fornication, uncleanness, inordinate affection, evil concupiscence, and covetousness which is idolatry," (Colossians 3:5). Every sin they see, they look on with an eye of grief and hatred, and strike at it.

5. Those who are heirs to the crown of life have their fruit unto holiness. "But now being made free from sin, and become the servants of God, ye have your fruit unto holiness, and the end everlasting life," (Romans 6:22). "The pure in heart shall see the Lord," (Matthew 5:8) his back parts now,

his face in glory. And truly the holy are only fit to behold the Holy One. Are you an enemy to holiness? You are an enemy to your own life. The heirs of this life understand that Jerusalem above is a holy city; therefore they apply and plead the promise of sanctification; they cleanse themselves from all filthiness of the flesh and spirit, perfecting holiness in the fear of God, (2 Corinthians 7:1).

6. Those who are heirs to the crown of life persevere to the end; they are faithful to the end, as the text speaks; they hold fast what they have, that none may take their crown away; they not only begin, but finish their course, and keep the faith, and so they receive a crown of righteousness at the hands of the Lord, the righteous Judge.

Use 3. Suffer. I beseech you a few words of exhortation, and I shall conclude with them.

1. Let the serious and believing consideration of this crown of life enliven and quicken you to every duty. Are you hearing for a crown and praying for worldly treasure, and will you hear carelessly and pray coldly? Does not such a kingdom as heaven is, deserve that you should use a holy violence to take it? Why slothful and dead when such glory is in view? O strive to enter in at the strait gate, that when you seek to enter in at heaven's door, and cryest "Lord, Lord, open to me," entrance may not be denied.

2. Let this crown of life be made use of to silence Satan

and to fence you against temptation. When the devil tells you of the ease and gain and pleasure, which sin will afford, reply, "Come O thou lying and deceitful spirit, put your ease and gain and pleasure into one balance, of the sanctuary, and I will put the crown of life and glory into the other, and what is sinful ease to the saints rest? Or the gain of gold, to the saints glory? Or pleasures for a moment, to eternal rejoicing? Satan will not know what to say to this, but perceiving unlikelihood of prevailing will flee from you.

3. Let this crown of life loosen your hearts from the world. Do not defile and load yourselves with thick clay, do not stick fast therein, when such glory is so certain and near at hand. Do not be desirous of, or content with a portion in this life, since you are just entering on a better one. Live as strangers and pilgrims on earth, and declare plainly that you seek a better country than the world has.

4. Let this crown of life, steal your hearts against suffering. Do not fear what enemies can do, since the keys of heaven do not hang at their girdle, nor glory is given of their pleasure. Our Lord set the joy before him so he endured the cross and despised the shame, (Hebrews 12:2); and if you imitate him, you shall at length sit down where he is at the right hand of the throne of God.

5. Let this crown of life set you above the fear of dissolution; it cannot be enjoyed until you are gone from here,

you must die before you can live the life above. Let your death be natural or violent, you must not be startled or amazed. The angels are ready to do their office, to convey you to paradise. Christ's arms are open to receive you, which are part of his purchase, and his redeemed ones. Christ understands what it is to die, it is an unusual trial, which you can have experience of only once; unusual strength shall be afforded. If death was only looked on as a dark passage into the glorious and lightsome inheritance, it would be no longer terrible, but desirable.

6. Let this crown of life make you long for your Lord's appearing. O cry to him to remove time and days out of the way, and that the wheels of his chariot may make greater haste. Long for the time when the heavens shall break asunder, and the fairest of ten thousand shall show his face through the clouds, and sit on his great white throne to judge the world in righteousness. When he comes, "his reward will be with him," (Revelation 22:12). Never a saint shall be seen without a crown at that day. And O what a spectacle it will be to behold the Head, and all the members together! Every one having on a rich and sparkling diadem! The saints are described to be such as love their Lord's appearing. And there is reason that they should wish for it. For when Christ who is their life shall appear, then shall they also appear with him in glory.

FINIS

www.ingramcontent.com/pod-product-compliance
Lightning Source LLC
Chambersburg PA
CBHW032002080426
42735CB00007B/484